JONAH AND THE BIG FISH

Activity Book

Jonah and the Big Fish Activity Book

All rights reserved. By purchasing this Activity Book, the buyer is permitted to copy the activity sheets for personal and classroom use only, but not for commercial resale. With the exception of the above, this Activity Book may not be reproduced in whole or in part in any manner without written permission of the publisher.

Bible Pathway Adventures® is a trademark of BPA Publishing Ltd.
Defenders of the Faith® is a trademark of BPA Publishing Ltd.

ISBN: 978-1-7771601-5-9

Author: Pip Reid
Creative Director: Curtis Reid

For more Bible resources, including Activity Books and printables, visit our website at:

www.biblepathwayadventures.com

◦◊ Introduction ◊◦

Welcome to the Jonah and the Big Fish Activity Book! This engaging educational resource is designed to bring the story of Jonah to life with ready-to-go lesson plans and fun activities for elementary students. Inside, you'll find interactive worksheets that guide children through key events in Jonah's story, such as his attempt to escape from God, the storm at sea, being swallowed by a fish, Nineveh's repentance, and Jonah's encounter with the plant. Perfect for use in classrooms, at home, or in children's ministries, each lesson encourages creativity, critical thinking, and a deeper understanding of Jonah's story.

Bible Pathway Adventures helps educators teach children the Biblical faith in a fun and creative way. We do this via our Activity Books and free printable activities – available on our website: www.biblepathwayadventures.com

Thanks for buying this Activity Book and supporting our ministry. Every book purchased helps us continue our work providing free Classroom Packs and discipleship resources to families and missions around the world.

The search for Truth is more fun than Tradition!

◆◇◆ Table of Contents ◆◇◆

Introduction 3

Lesson One: The runaway prophet 6
Coloring page: Jonah the prophet 8
Bible word search puzzle: The runaway prophet 9
Worksheet: The port of Joppa 10
Map activity: The Assyrian Empire 11
Worksheet: What's the Word? 12
Worksheet: Jonah runs from God 13
Worksheet: The world's traders 14
Bible craft: Make a paper boat 15
Let's learn Hebrew: Jonah 16
Worksheet: Discovering the tribe of Zebulun 18
Worksheet: The land of Zebulun 19

Lesson Two: Storm at sea 20
Bible quiz: Jonah and the mighty storm 22
Bible verse puzzle: Who was Jonah? 23
Newspaper worksheet: The Bible Times 24
Worksheet: The runaway prophet 25
Worksheet: Who were the Phoenicians? 26
Map activity: Design your own trading route 27
Worksheet: My Phoenician trade journal 28
Coloring page: Casting lots 29
Creative writing: Overboard! 30
Let's learn Hebrew: The Hebrew alphabet 31

Lesson Three: Swallowed by a fish 34
Coloring page: Swallowed by a fish 36
Bible word search puzzle: Swallowed by a fish 37
Worksheet: Parts of a fish 38
Let's learn Hebrew: Fish 39
Worksheet: Swallowed by a fish 40
Worksheet: Understanding the Hebrew day 41
Coloring worksheet: Jonah and the great fish 42

Worksheet: Who was Jonah?..43
Labyrinth: To Nineveh!..44
Worksheet: City of Nineveh...45

Lesson Four: Nineveh repents.. 46
Coloring page: The king of Nineveh repents..48
Bible quiz: God's message to Nineveh...49
Bible word scramble: How big was Nineveh?...50
Worksheet: Who was the King of Nineveh?..51
Worksheet: Write your name in cuneiform 52
Bible activity: Ancient Nineveh 53
Worksheet: Sackcloth and ashes..54
Worksheet: Repentance in action...55
Coloring activity: Discovering the Assyrian King..56
Worksheet: Meet the cast...57

Lesson Five: Jonah and the plant 58
Coloring page: Jonah and the plant..60
Newspaper worksheet: Nineveh repents! 61
Bible crossword puzzle: Jonah in Nineveh..62
Worksheet: From shade to sun...63
Let's learn Hebrew: Tola'at...64
Worksheet: Design a worm..65
Worksheet: Exploring mercy..66
Bible quiz: Jonah and the big fish 67
Story sequencing activity: Jonah's big adventure 68
Worksheet: True or false?...69
Bible story worksheets: Write your own story of Jonah 70

Bible story cards: The story of Jonah..74

Crafts & Projects
Bible activity: Jonah sails to Tarshish...81
Bible craft: Make a rain cloud 83
Worksheet: How do plants grow?...89
Bible activity: God is merciful..91

Answer Key 93
Discover more Activity Books! 97

LESSON ONE

The runaway prophet: Jonah 1:1-3

1. Lesson objectives:

During this lesson, children will explore:
1. Why God asked Jonah to go to Nineveh
2. Why Jonah tried to run away from God

2. Introduction:

To start the lesson, engage students by asking if they've ever avoided doing something they were supposed to do. Invite some of them to share their stories and the outcomes. Then, explain that today's lesson will begin to explore the story of Jonah, a prophet who tried to run away from God's instructions. Emphasize that as they read Jonah 1:1-3, they should think about why it's important to obey God, even when it's challenging. Encourage them to consider what happens when Jonah decides to go his own way instead of following God's plan.

3. Review key vocabulary:

- **JONAH:** An Israelite prophet chosen by God to deliver messages from Him
- **NINEVEH:** A city in ancient Assyria
- **TARSHISH:** A faraway place Jonah tried to escape to
- **PROPHET:** A person called by God to speak on His behalf
- **JOPPA (JAFFA):** A port city on the Mediterranean Sea where Jonah boarded a ship

4. Bible memory verse to help children remember God's Word:

"Arise, go to Nineveh, that great city, and call out against it, for their evil has come up before Me." (Jonah 1:2)

5. Read Jonah 1:1-3 or read the Bible story below:

One day, God spoke to Jonah, the son of Amittai. He said, "Get up and go to Nineveh, that big city, and tell the people there to repent (turn to Me and follow My Ways) because I have seen their evil actions." But instead of listening to God, Jonah decided to run away. He went down to the city of Joppa and found a ship that was going to a place called Tarshish. Jonah paid for his ticket and got on the ship, hoping to escape from God's presence.

6. Let's review:

1. What was today's story about?
2. Who did God speak to in the story?
3. What did God tell Jonah to do?
4. Where did Jonah go instead of Nineveh?
5. Why did Jonah decide to run away from God?
6. What is a prophet?

7. Activites:

* Coloring page: Jonah the prophet
* Bible word search puzzle: The runaway prophet
* Worksheet: The port of Joppa
* Map activity: The Assyrian Empire
* Worksheet: What's the Word?
* Worksheet: Jonah runs from God
* Bible activity: Jonah sails to Tarshish
* Worksheet: The world's traders
* Bible craft: Make a paper boat
* Let's learn Hebrew: Jonah
* Worksheet: Discovering the tribe of Zebulun
* Worksheet: The land of Zebulun

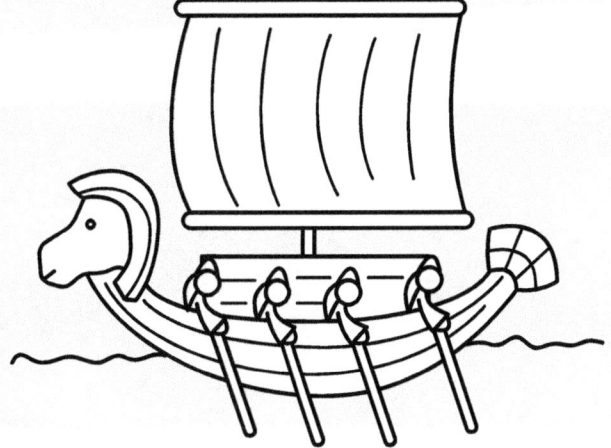

"**Arise, go to Nineveh, that great city, and call out against it.**"

(Jonah 1:2)

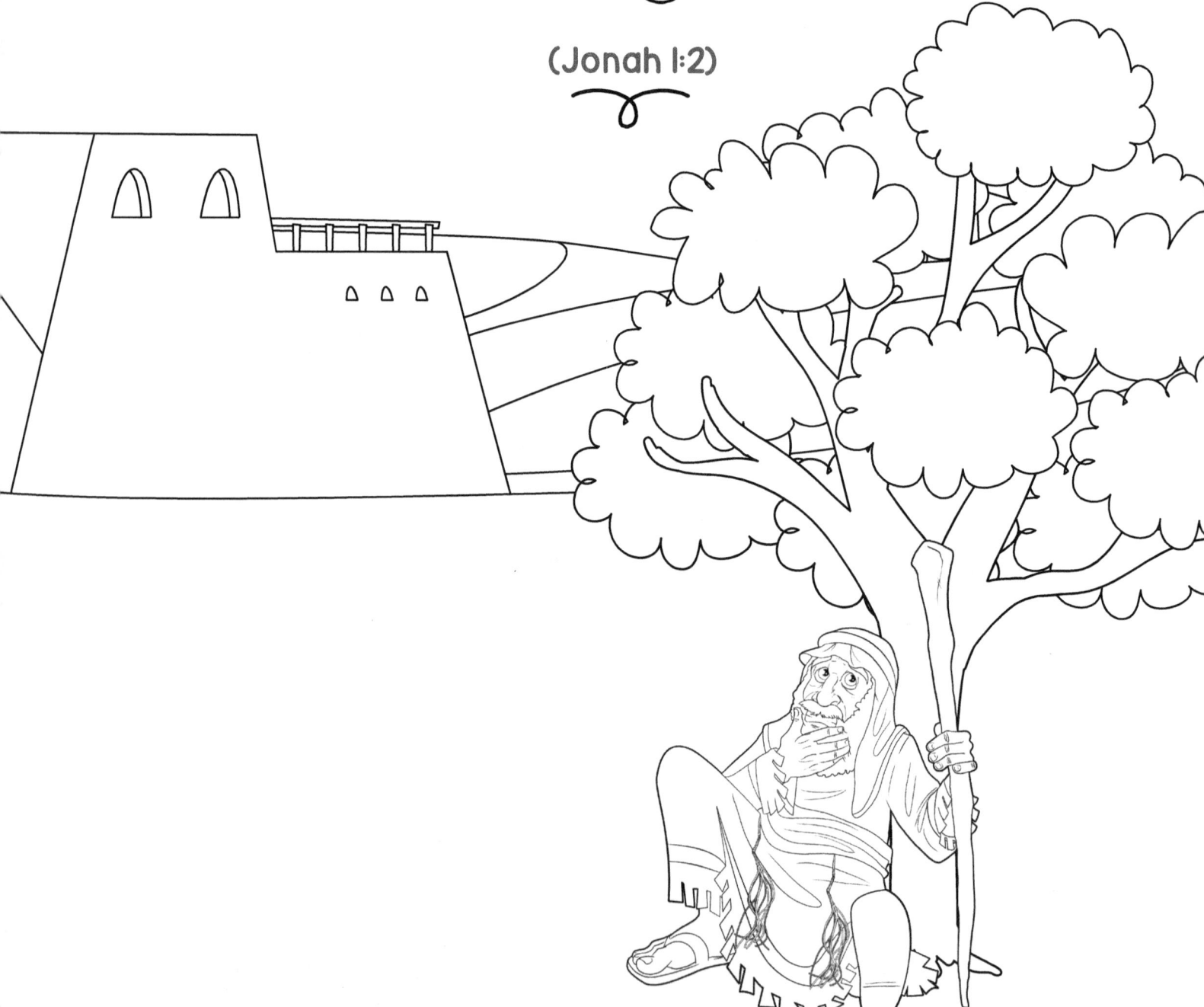

The runaway PROPHET

Read Jonah 1:1-3. Find and circle the words below.

```
R A K J G S S L Z M W P G X J
D Z M O G M N D N K J R C B B
D K H I N J I H Z V N E K S F
P Z Y A T B S D P L X S S E A
E V U T W T R S Z S B E A O R
N L H K A U A E I H Q N R F E
C I T Y H H E I R Z K C J L H
F M U U N D L Q K P M E O H N
G J C O R G I K N M P Q P F I
P Y O A Q J T R G H S O P J N
J Z D N W P E Z G D A J A V E
H M E M A H E B R E W C G T V
V T A R S H I S H J P O V U E
V M A X D D P R O P H E T L H
H V Z F L G W S H I P L U B I
```

HEBREW

SHIP

CITY

PROPHET

JOPPA

TARSHISH

JONAH

ISRAELITE

PRESENCE

AMITTAI

NINEVEH

FARE

The port of Joppa

The Phoenicians were expert sailors and traders in ancient times. They played a big role in connecting different cultures and places around the Mediterranean Sea. One important port they used was Joppa, which is known today as Jaffa. Joppa was located on the eastern Mediterranean coast and had a natural harbor, making it a perfect spot for ships to anchor safely. Joppa became a bustling hub for trade and travel because of the Phoenicians. They were very good at navigating the sea and setting up trade routes. These routes connected places like Egypt, Cyprus, and other important locations. The Phoenicians' skills and their use of Joppa helped them spread goods, ideas, and culture across great distances.

Jonah likely went to Joppa to find a ship heading to Tarshish. According to the Bible, Jonah was trying to run away from God's command to go to the city of Nineveh. He thought that by traveling to Tarshish, a faraway place, he could escape his mission. At Joppa, he would have found many Phoenician ships preparing for long voyages. The Phoenicians were known for their long-distance travels, and their ships were capable of sailing great distances across the Mediterranean Sea. The experienced and skilled Phoenician sailors made Joppa the perfect place for Jonah to start his journey. Thanks to the Phoenicians, Joppa was a well-known and busy port that played a key role in connecting different parts of the ancient world.

1. What made Joppa an ideal port for the Phoenicians to use for their trade and travel?

2. Why do you think Jonah likely chose to go to Joppa to find a ship?

3. How did the Phoenicians' skills in navigation and trade contribute to their influence across the Mediterranean Sea?

The Assyrian Empire

Nineveh was the capital of the Assyrian Empire from 705 to 612 B.C. Find and mark the boundaries of the Assyrian Empire on the map. Add the places in the map key to the map. You may need to use the Internet or a historical atlas to find the answers.

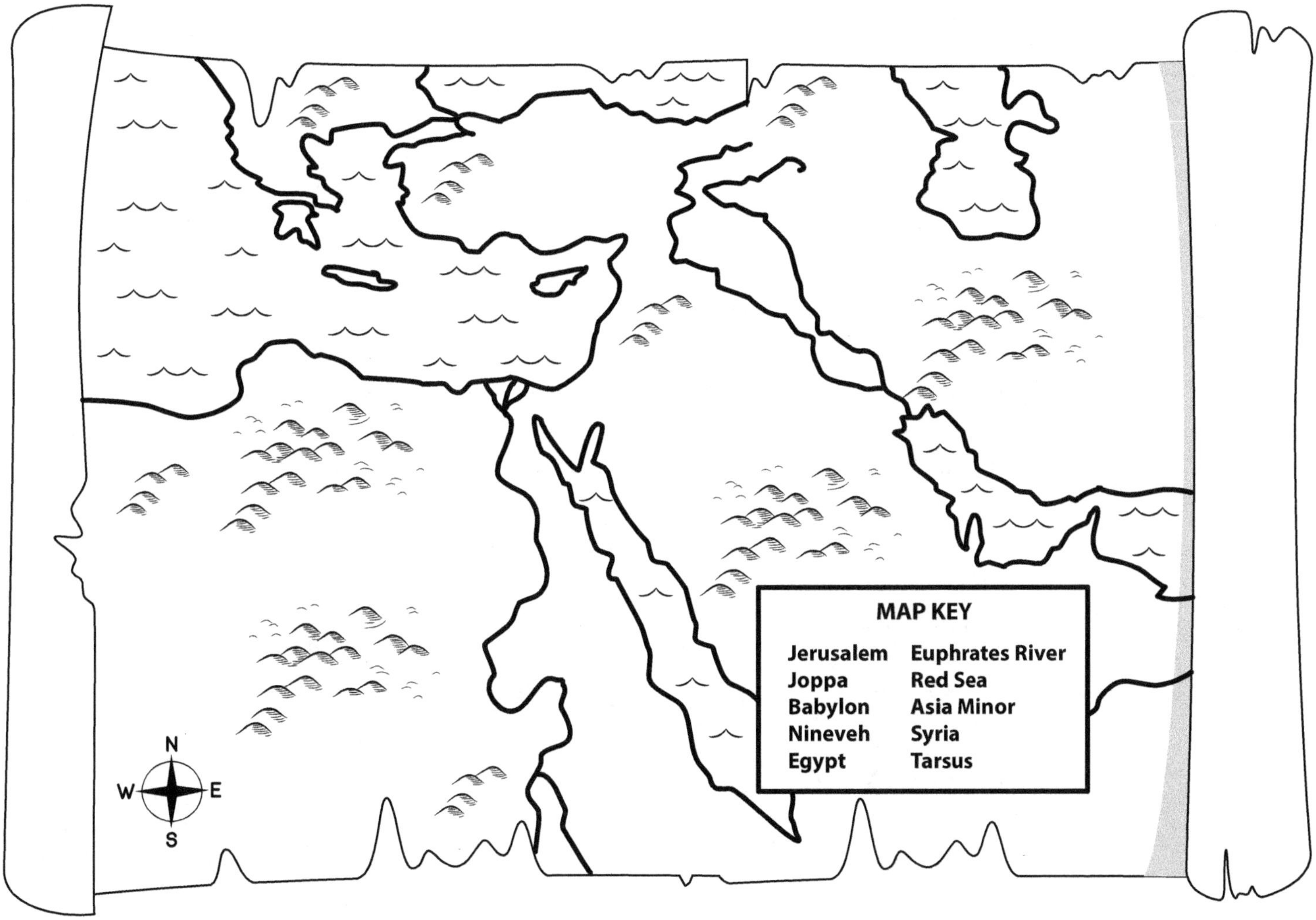

MAP KEY

Jerusalem	Euphrates River
Joppa	Red Sea
Babylon	Asia Minor
Nineveh	Syria
Egypt	Tarsus

What's the Word?

Read Jonah 1:1-4. Using the words below,
fill in the blanks to complete the Bible passage.

| JONAH | AMITTAI | SHIP | JOPPA | TARSHISH |
| NINEVEH | FLEE | VIOLENT | WICKEDNESS | PORT |

"The word of Yahweh came to ...., son of ....: "Go to the great city of .... and preach against it, because its .... has come up before Me." But Jonah ran away from God and headed for .... He went down to .... where he found a .... bound for that .... After paying the fare, he went aboard and sailed for Tarshish to .... from God. Then God sent a great wind on the sea, and such a .... storm arose that the ship threatened to break up."

Jonah runs from God

God gave Jonah some important instructions. Did Jonah obey Him?
Read Jonah 1:1-3 and write God's instructions to Jonah below.

Answer the questions below.

| Why did God tell Jonah to go to Nineveh? | Why do you think Jonah disobeyed God? | Where did Jonah board a ship? |

The world's traders

At the time of Jonah, the Phoenicians were the world's most advanced sailors and traders. They based themselves in coastal cities such as Tyre and Sidon and sailed across the Mediterranean, Atlantic, Red Sea, and Indian Ocean to trade with other nations and cultures. It is quite possible that Jonah boarded a Phoenician ship when he tried to run away from God. Using the Internet or an encyclopedia, research what goods the Phoenicians exported to other countries. Write them in the boxes below.

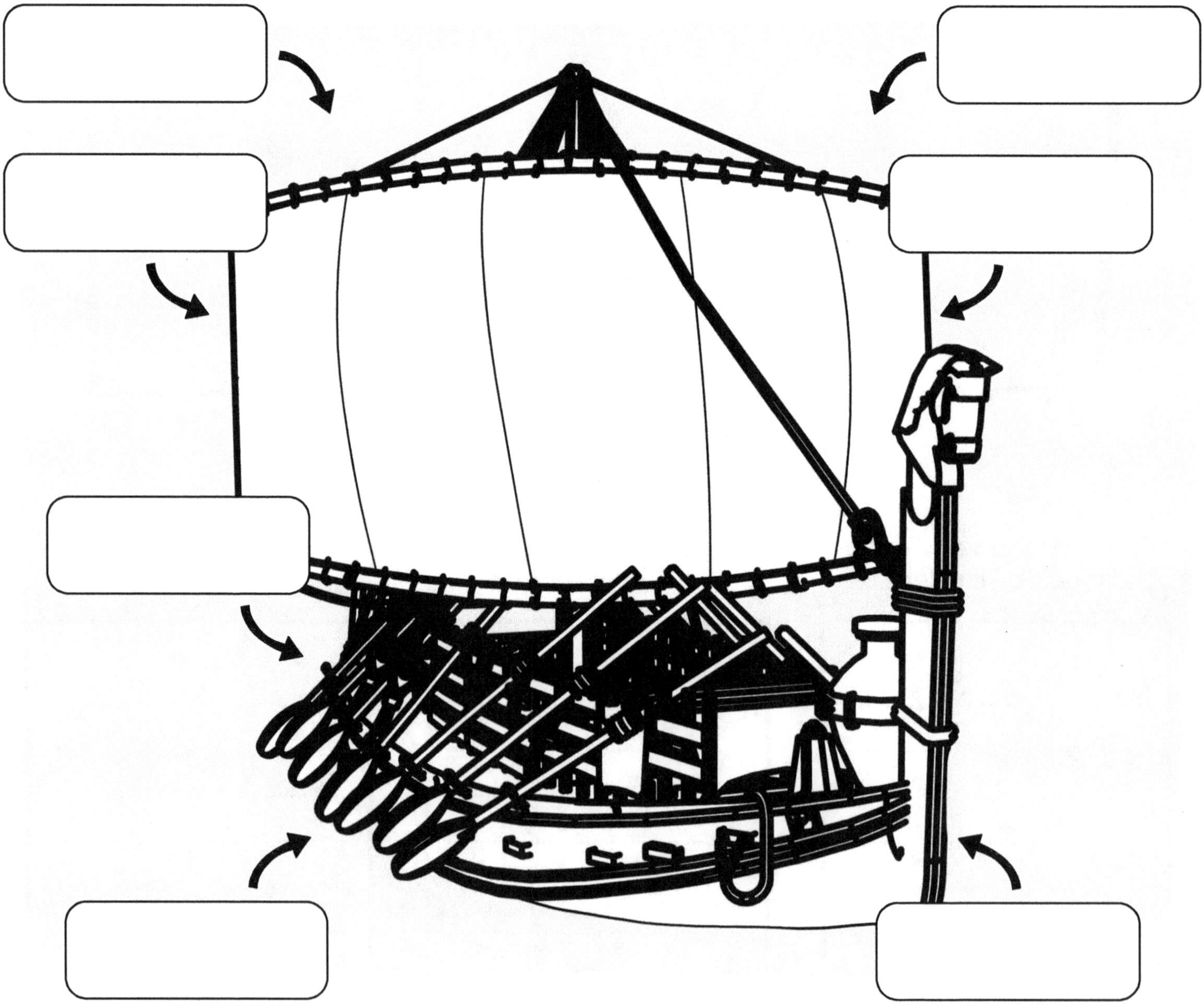

www.biblepathwayadventures.com
Jonah and the Big Fish Activity Book

© BPA Publishing Ltd 2024

Sail away!

In the story of Jonah, he tried to flee from God by boarding a ship. Now, you can create your very own paper boat and imagine the adventures Jonah might have had on the sea.

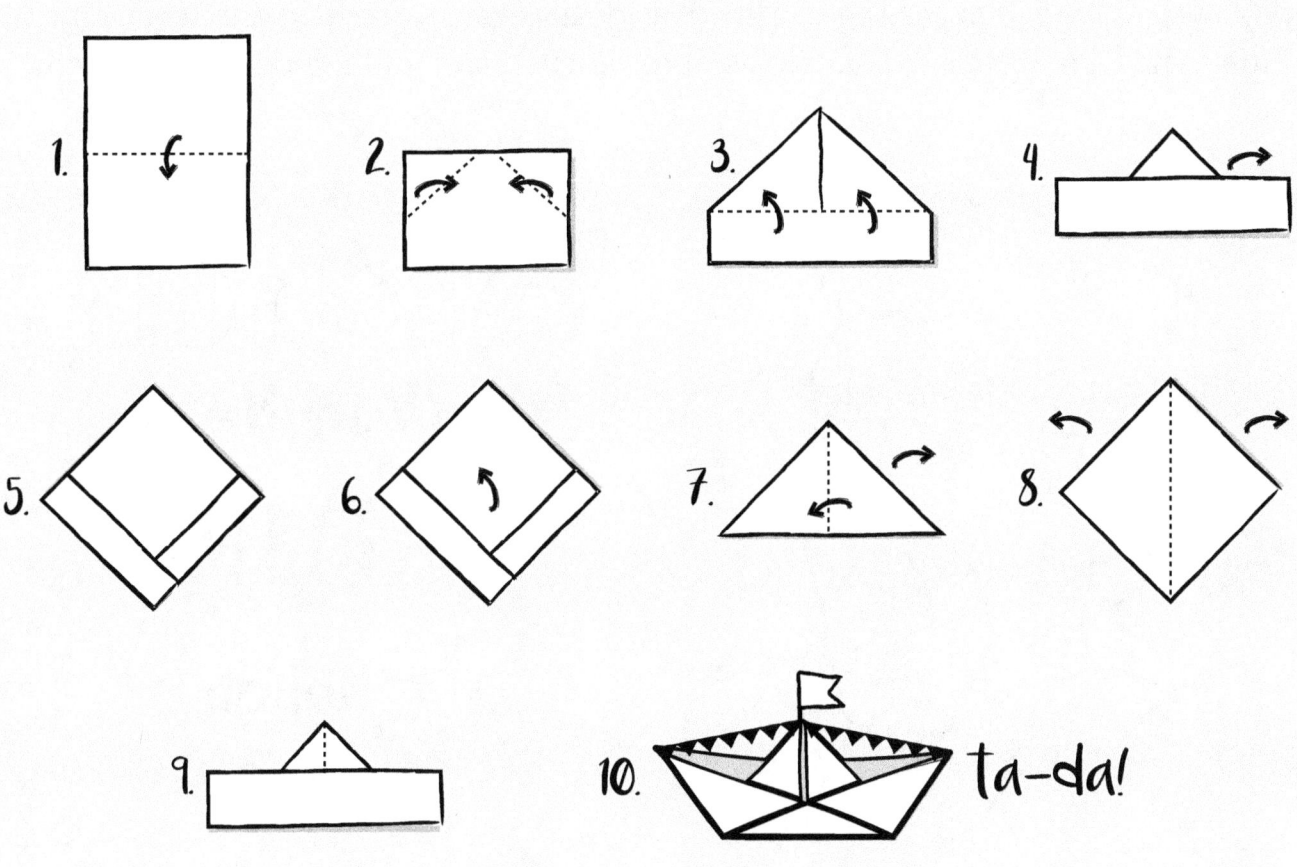

1. Fold a piece of paper (A4 or letter size) in half from top to bottom.
2. Fold the top corners in towards the middle so that they meet. Leave 1-2 inches of space at the bottom.
3. Fold the flaps at the bottom of the triangle shape up on both sides.
4. Pop out the middle to make a hat shape.
5. Open the hat shape out even more until it forms a square. Tuck the corners of one flap under the other.
6. Fold up the bottom flaps of the square on both sides so you have a triangle shape.
7. Pull out the middle of the triangle to form a square.
8. Pull out the middle of the square, and press the shape flat.
9. Open out from the bottom to create your boat shape.

Yonah

The Hebrew name for Jonah is Yonah. He was a Hebrew prophet of the northern kingdom of Israel in about the 8th century BC. God told him to go to Nineveh and tell the people to repent. Instead, he ran away and went in a ship to Tarshish. After God sent a storm, Jonah was thrown into the sea. He lived inside a fish for three days and three nights. Finally, he turned back to God. He went to Nineveh and told the people to repent.

Yonah
(Yoh-NAH)

יוֹנָה

Jonah

Trace the Hebrew name here:

יונה

יונה

Write the Hebrew name here:

Let's write!

Practice writing Jonah's Hebrew name on the lines below.

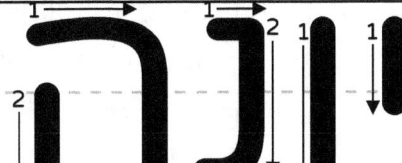

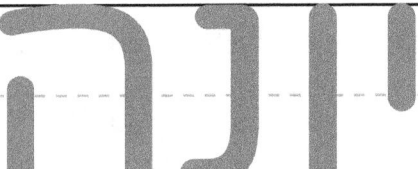

Try this on your own.
Remember that Hebrew is read from RIGHT to LEFT.

Discovering the tribe of Zebulun

The Hebrew name for Zebulun is Zevulun. Zebulun was the tenth son of Jacob (Israel). Jacob blessed Zebulun, saying, "You will live by the sea and be a safe place for ships" (Genesis 49:13). The tribe of Zebulun was given a small portion of southern Galilee, between Asher and Naphtali. In Judges 5, Deborah praised this tribe for risking their lives. Yeshua began His ministry in Galilee, fulfilling Isaiah's prophecy in Isaiah 9 and Matthew 4. They were known for their bravery and skills in battle. One notable person from the tribe was Elon, a judge of Israel (Judges 12). Jonah, the prophet who tried to flee from God, was from Gath-hepher, a town in Zebulun's territory (2 Kings 14).

Answer the questions below.

1. Who was Zebulun?

2. Where did the tribe of Zebulun settle?

3. Who was a famous prophet from the tribe of Zebulun?

4. What did Deborah praise the tribe of Zebulun for in Judges 5?

The symbol often associated with Zebulun is a ship. Draw a ship on the banner.

The land of Zebulun

Zebulun's land was important because it was a great place for trade and travel. The tribe's territory included fertile land for farming and was close to important trade routes. This helped them exchange goods and ideas with other cultures. Zebulun's land was also significant in the life of Yeshua. The region of Galilee, where Zebulun was located, is where He began His ministry. This fulfilled a prophecy from the book of Isaiah, showing the lasting importance of Zebulun's territory in biblical history.
Circle Jonah's hometown on the map below. Color the map.

Read Judges 5 and 12, 1 Chronicles 12, Isaiah 9, and Matthew 4. Why was the tribe of Zebulun significant in the history of Israel?

....

....

....

LESSON TWO

Storm at sea: Jonah 1:4-16

1. Lesson objectives:

During this lesson, children will explore:
1. Why God sent a storm on the sea
2. What the sailors did to stop the storm and save the ship from sinking

2. Introduction:

To start the lesson, ask your students if they enjoy playing "Hide and Seek." Discuss how fun it is to find a great hiding spot. Explain that they will play a quick game of hide and seek with a twist. Choose one student to be the seeker while the others hide. After the game, discuss how it would feel if the seeker always knew their hiding spots. Say, "Our lesson today is about Jonah, who, as you all know, tried to hide from God. Just like in our game, no matter where Jonah hid, God knew exactly where he was."

3. Review key vocabulary:

- **SAILORS:** People who work on a ship and help sail it across the sea

- **CAPTAIN:** The person in charge of a ship or boat

- **CARGO:** The goods or items that are carried on a ship, airplane, or truck

- **HEBREW:** A person from one of the 12 tribes of Israel. It's also the name of their language

- **PERISH:** To die or be destroyed, especially in a sudden or unexpected way

4. Bible memory verse to help children remember God's Word:

"I am a Hebrew, and I fear Yahweh, the God of heaven, who made the sea and the dry land." (Jonah 1:9)

5. Read Jonah 1:4-16 or read the Bible story below:

God sent a powerful wind that caused a huge storm on the sea. The ship Jonah was on began to break apart. The sailors were scared and each cried out to their own god. They threw the ship's cargo into the sea to make the ship lighter. But Jonah had gone below deck and was fast asleep. The captain found him and said, "How can you sleep? Get up and call on your god! Maybe he will save us, so we won't die." The sailors decided to cast lots to find out who was responsible for the trouble. The lot fell on Jonah. They asked him, "Who is to blame for this disaster? What do you do? Where are you from?" Jonah answered, "I am a Hebrew, and I worship Yahweh, the God of heaven, who made the sea and the land." The sailors were terrified and asked, "What have you done?" They knew he was running away from the Lord because he had told them. The sea was getting rougher, so they asked Jonah, "What should we do to make the sea calm down?" Jonah replied, "Throw me into the sea, and it will become calm. I know it is my fault this storm has come upon you." The sailors tried to row back to land, but they couldn't because the sea grew even wilder. They cried out to God, "Please don't let us die because of this man's life. Don't hold us accountable for killing an innocent man, for You have done as you pleased." Then they took Jonah and threw him overboard, and the sea became calm. The sailors were filled with great awe and offered a sacrifice to God and made vows to Him.

6. Let's review:

1. What was today's story about?
2. Why did God send a storm on the sea?
3. How did the sailors react to the storm?
4. Where was Jonah when the storm hit the ship?
5. What did the captain say to Jonah when he found him asleep?
6. How did the sailors decide who was responsible for the storm?
7. What did Jonah tell the sailors about himself and why the storm had come?
8. What did Jonah tell the sailors to do to calm the storm, and what happened when they did it?

7. Activites:

* Bible quiz: Jonah and the mighty storm
* Bible verse puzzle: Who was Jonah?
* Newspaper worksheet: The Bible Times
* Worksheet: The runaway prophet
* Worksheet: Who were the Phoenicians?
* Map activity: Design your own trading route
* Worksheet: My Phoenician trade journal
* Coloring page: Casting lots
* Creative writing: Overboard!
* Let's learn Hebrew: The Hebrew alphabet
* Bible craft: Make a rain cloud

Jonah and the MIGHTY STORM

Read Jonah 1:4-16. Answer the questions below.

1. What caused the ship to be in danger?

2. How did the mariners (sailors) react to the storm?

3. What did the sailors do to try to lighten the ship?

4. Where was Jonah during the storm?

5. What did the captain say to Jonah when he found him asleep?

6. How did the sailors decide who was responsible for the storm?

7. What did Jonah tell the sailors about himself?

8. Why were the sailors afraid when Jonah told them who he was?

9. What did Jonah suggest the sailors do to calm the storm?

10. What happened after the sailors threw Jonah into the sea?

Who was Jonah?

This Bible verse is written in code. Use the chart at the bottom of the page to fill in the missing letters and crack the code! *Hint: Read Jonah 1:9 (ESV)*

$\frac{}{6}\frac{}{2}\frac{}{21}\ \frac{}{2}\ \frac{E}{17}\frac{}{22}\frac{}{14}\frac{E}{10}\frac{}{22}\frac{}{24},\ \frac{}{2}\frac{D}{4}\frac{}{8}\ \frac{}{6}\frac{}{23}\frac{E}{22}\frac{}{2}\frac{}{10}$

$\frac{}{16}\frac{}{17}\frac{E}{22}\frac{}{20}\frac{}{7}\frac{}{10}\frac{D}{8},\ \frac{}{16}\frac{}{17}\frac{E}{22}\ \frac{}{25}\frac{D}{7}\frac{}{8}\ \frac{}{7}\frac{}{23}\frac{}{17}\frac{E}{22}\frac{}{2}\frac{V}{11}\frac{E}{22}\frac{}{4},$

$\frac{}{24}\frac{}{17}\frac{}{7}\ \frac{}{21}\frac{D}{2}\frac{E}{8}\frac{}{22}\ \frac{}{16}\frac{}{17}\frac{E}{22}\ \frac{S}{19}\frac{E}{22}\frac{}{2}\ \frac{}{2}\frac{D}{4}\frac{}{8}$

$\frac{}{16}\frac{}{17}\frac{E}{22}\ \frac{D}{8}\frac{}{10}\frac{}{18}\frac{}{20}\frac{}{2}\frac{D}{4}\frac{}{8}.$

A	B	C	D	E	F	G	H	I	J	K	L	M
			8	22								

N	O	P	Q	R	S	T	U	V	W	X	Y	Z
					19			11				

City of Joppa

The Bible Times

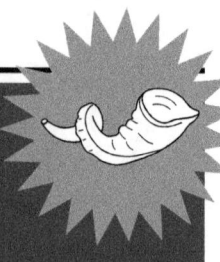

LAND OF ISRAEL A BIBLE HISTORY PUBLICATION

Great Storm Hits Ship

Sailors Toss Jonah Overboard

....

....

....

....

....

Missing Cargo

The runaway prophet

To get away from the presence of God, Jonah boarded a ship to Tarshish (Jonah 1:3). What do you think he took with him? Think about life in ancient Israel. Use your imagination and draw some items inside the suitcase.

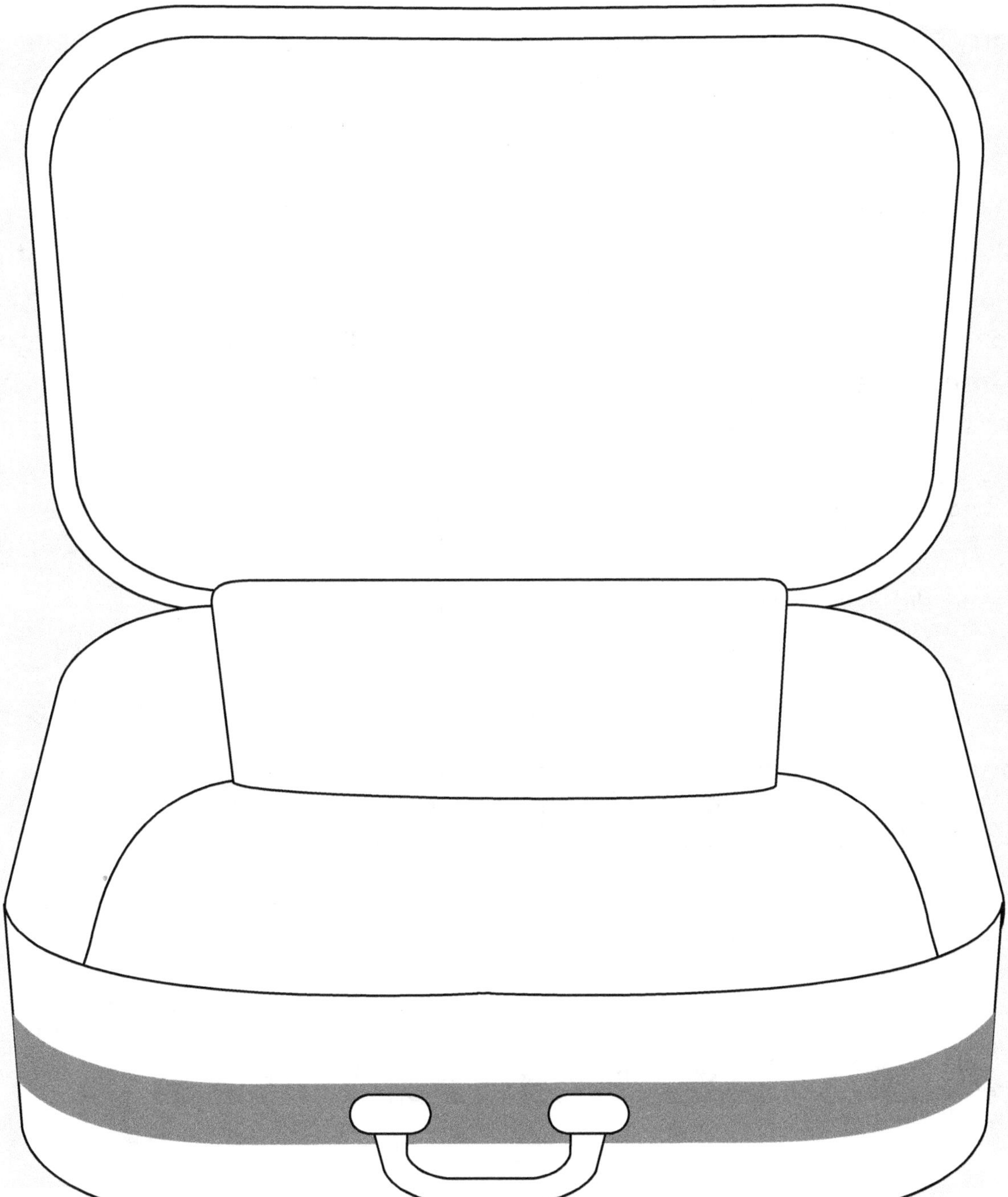

Who were the Phoenicians?

Phoenicia was an ancient civilization located along the coasts of modern Lebanon and Syria. From 1500 BC to 300 BC, the Phoenicians were the world's best sailors and traders. They lived in coastal cities like Tyre and Sidon and traveled across the Mediterranean Sea, the Atlantic Ocean, the Red Sea, and the Indian Ocean to trade with other countries. Their ships were very large, able to carry up to 600 passengers and lots of cargo. Jonah likely boarded a Phoenician ship in the port of Joppa (modern-day Jaffa). The Phoenicians were known for their excellent seafaring skills, and Joppa was a key port for their trading activities.

Some historians think the Phoenicians might have discovered North America long before Christopher Columbus. They have found old writing, ancient copper mines, and other signs of Phoenician influence in North America. For example, on Monhegan Island, which is ten miles off the coast of Maine, there's an inscription written in Celtic Ogam that says, "Cargo platforms for ships from Phoenicia." Based on these findings and studies of the Phoenicians' sailing skills, some historians believe there was a trade route between America and the Mediterranean.

1. Where did Jonah likely board a Phoenician ship?

2. Do you think the evidence found by historians is enough to prove that the Phoenicians discovered North America before Christopher Columbus? Why or why not?

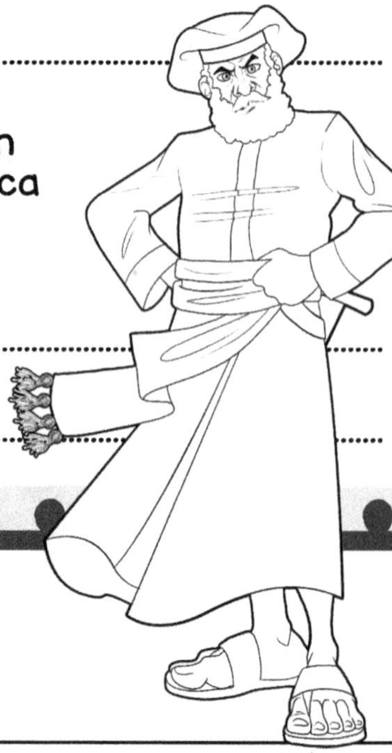

Design your own trading route

The Phoenicians were excellent traders and skilled navigators. They traveled widely and set up colonies wherever they went. Major trade routes included the Greek islands, southern Europe, the Atlantic coast of Africa, and ancient Britain. Their civilization first developed in the Levant, an area that today includes Lebanon, Syria, and Israel. Starting from the 10th century B.C., the Phoenicians expanded from their homeland and colonized territories throughout the Mediterranean. Trade and the search for valuable goods led to the creation of trading posts. Over time, these posts grew into larger cities and colonies. Imagine you are a Phoenician trader. Where would you sail to trade your goods? On the map provided, draw a line showing your trading route from Tyre to three other places you would like to visit. Name the places.

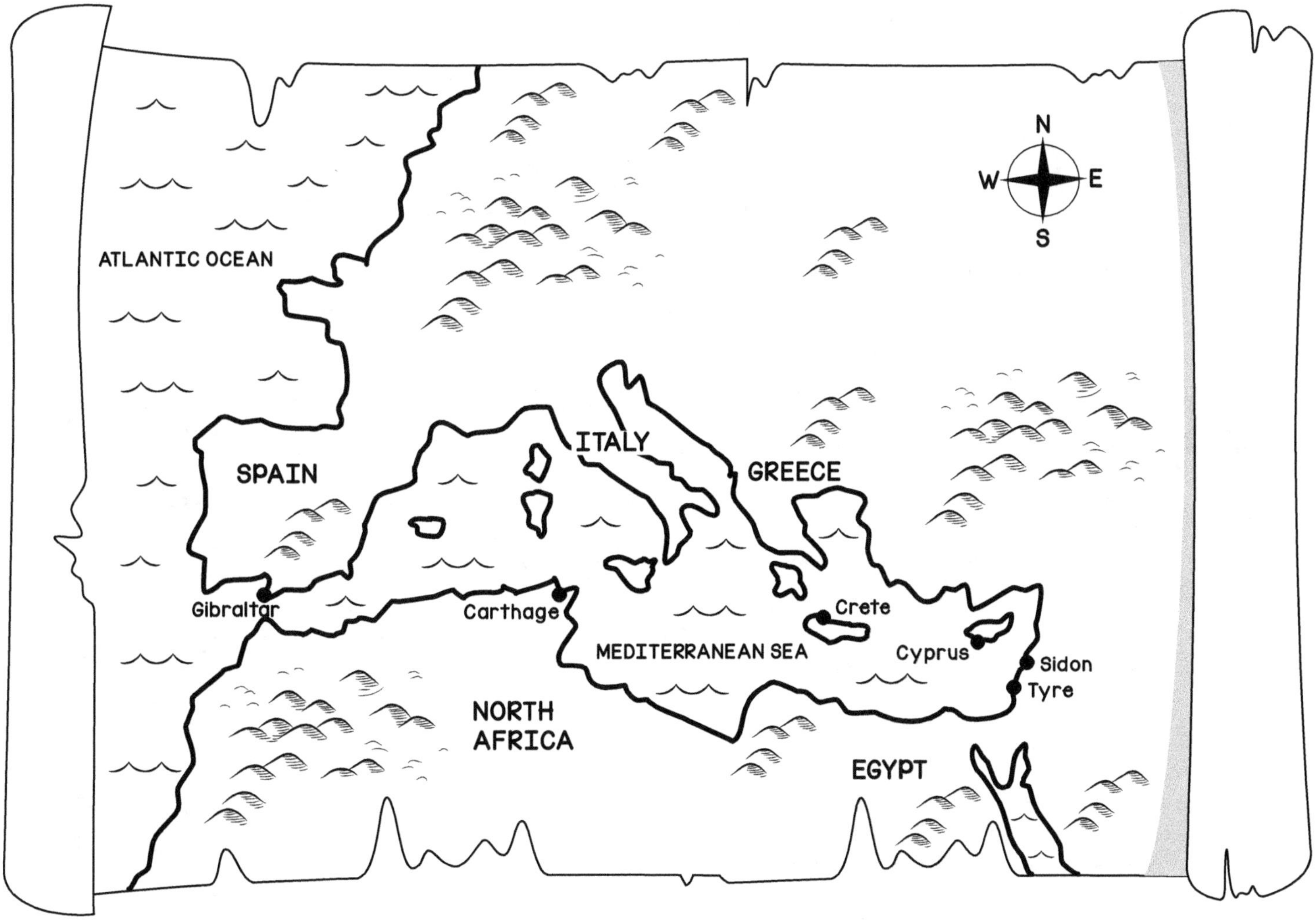

A Phoenician ship

Create a Phoenician ship by adding your own designs and color.

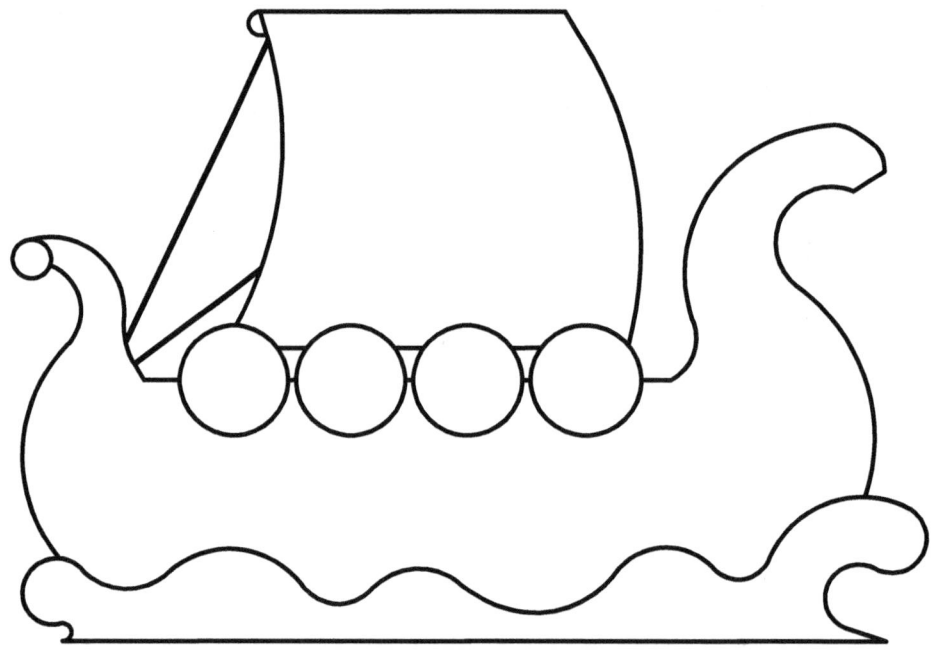

Pretend you are a Phoenician sailor. Write a short journal entry about your day. Describe what you see, the places you visit, and the people you meet. Include three items you are trading and explain why they are important.

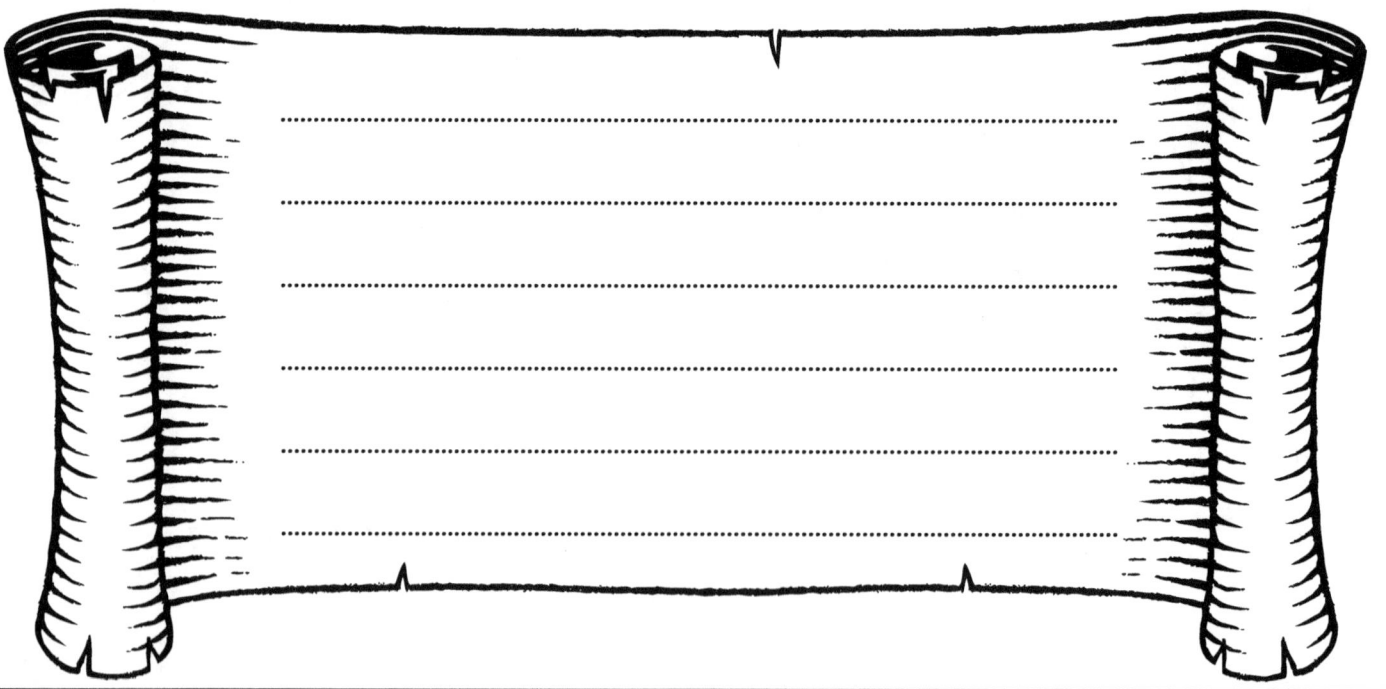

"They cast lots and the lot fell on Jonah."
(Jonah 1:7)

Overboard!

During a fierce storm, the sailors on Jonah's ship cast lots to find out who was causing the trouble, and the lot fell on Jonah. They asked him who he was, and he revealed that he was a Hebrew running away from God. Jonah told them to throw him into the sea to calm the storm. Despite their efforts to row back to land, the storm grew worse. The sailors prayed to God, asking not to be blamed for Jonah's death, then threw him overboard (Jonah 1:4-16). Write Jonah and the sailors' conversation in the speech bubbles below.

Let's learn Hebrew

Jonah was a Hebrew, a member of the ancient Israelite people. As a Hebrew, he likely spoke the Hebrew language, which was the language of his people. Hebrew has a unique alphabet with 22 letters, written from right to left. Learning the Hebrew alphabet can be exciting because it connects us to ancient history and the stories of the Israelites, like Jonah. Let's explore the Hebrew alphabet!

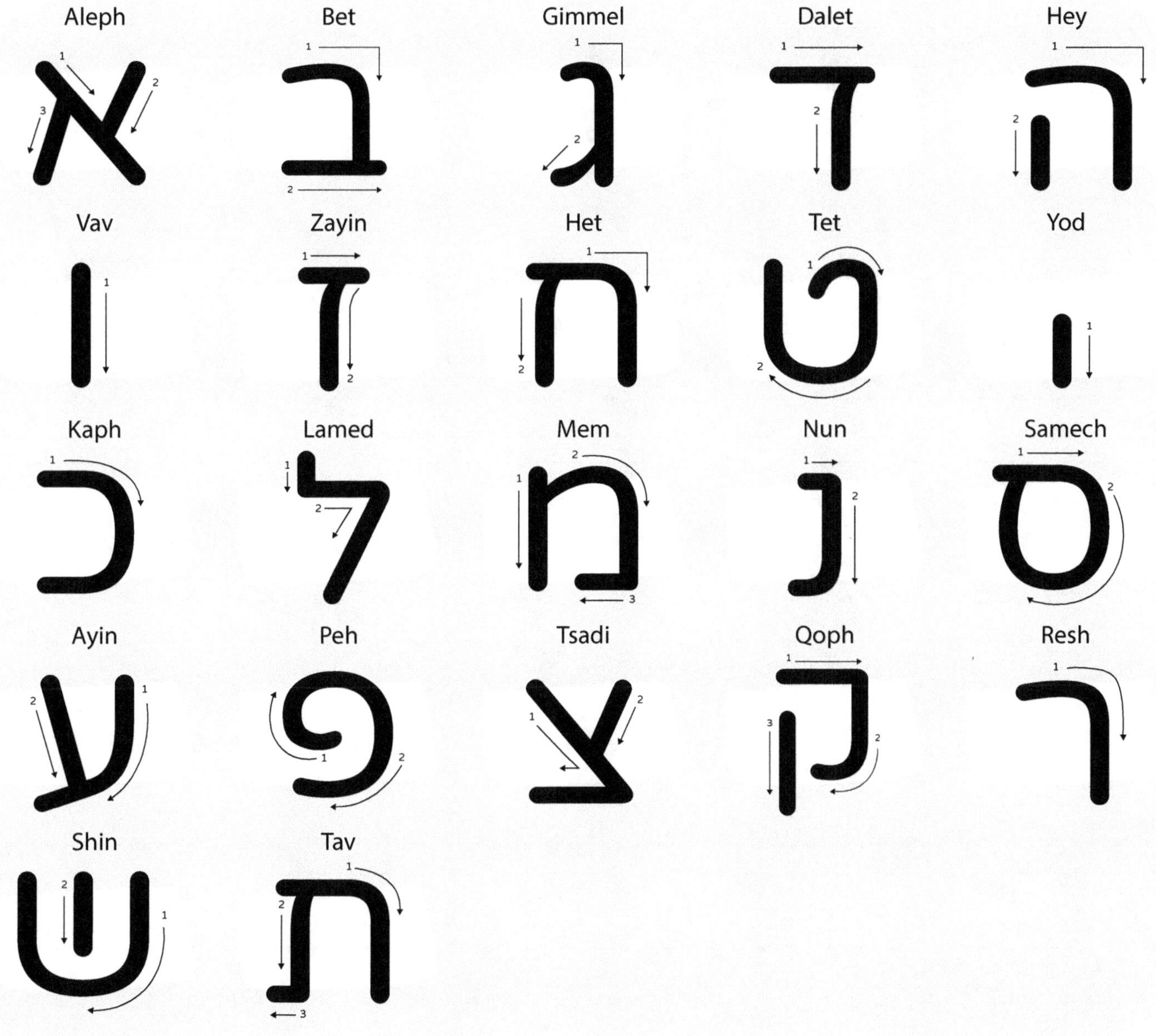

Aleph	Bet	Gimmel	Dalet	Hey
א	ב	ג	ד	ה

Vav	Zayin	Het	Tet	Yod
ו	ז	ח	ט	י

Kaph	Lamed	Mem	Nun	Samech
כ	ל	מ	נ	ס

Ayin	Peh	Tsadi	Qoph	Resh
ע	פ	צ	ק	ר

Shin	Tav
ש	ת

Practice writing these Hebrew letters on the lines below.
Remember that Hebrew is written from RIGHT to LEFT.

אבגדהוזחטיכל

Practice writing these Hebrew letters on the lines below.
Remember that Hebrew is written from RIGHT to LEFT.

ךלמהתנ

פעסנמל

קצףףעס

התשרק

LESSON THREE

Swallowed by a fish: Jonah 1:17-3:3

1. Lesson objectives:

During this lesson, children will explore:
1. How God dealt with Jonah by sending a great fish to save him
2. Why Jonah decided to repent and obey God's instructions

2. Introduction:

Begin the class by holding up a fish cut-out or a large fish toy. Say, "What would you do if a giant fish swallowed you every time you made an excuse to avoid doing something important?" Ask them to share their thoughts and reactions to engage them and get them thinking about the consequences of disobedience. Say, "Now, let's find out what happened to Jonah when he disobeyed God and how this story teaches us the importance of listening to and obeying God's commands."

3. Review key vocabulary:

- **SHEOL:** The place of the dead, where everyone goes to rest after they physically die

- **NINEVEH:** An ancient city in the Middle East

- **DISTRESS:** Extreme anxiety, sorrow or pain

- **THANKSGIVING:** An expression of gratitude to God

- **REPENTANCE:** Turning back to God and His Ways (Acts 26:20)

4. Bible memory verse to help children remember God's Word:

"God appointed a great fish to swallow up Jonah. Jonah was in the belly of the fish three days and three nights." (Jonah 1:17)

5. Read Jonah 1:17-3:3 or read the Bible story below:

As Jonah tumbled to the bottom of the sea, God sent a great fish to swallow him. Jonah was inside the fish for three days and three nights. While he was in the belly of the fish, Jonah prayed to God, and repented. He said, "When I was in trouble, I called out to God, and You answered me. I cried for help, and You heard my voice. You threw me into the deep sea, and the waves crashed over me. I thought I was driven away from Your sight, but I remembered God, and my prayer reached You." Jonah continued, "The waters surrounded me, and seaweed wrapped around my head. I sank down to the ocean floor, but You brought my life up from the pit. When I felt my life slipping away, I prayed to You. Those who worship idols lose their chance for steadfast love, but I will offer sacrifices to You with a thankful heart. Salvation belongs to God!" Then God commanded the fish to spit Jonah out onto dry land. "Jonah, go to Nineveh, that great city, and deliver the message I give you," said God. And so, Jonah hurried to Nineveh as fast as his legs could carry him.

6. Let's review:

1. What was today's story about?
2. How long was Jonah inside the belly of the fish?
3. What did Jonah do while he was inside the fish?
4. What did Jonah call out to God when he was in trouble?
5. What instructions did God give Jonah after three days and three nights?
6. Where did God send Jonah after he was spit out by the fish?

7. Activites:

* Coloring page: Swallowed by a fish
* Bible word search puzzle: Swallowed by a fish
* Worksheet: Parts of a fish
* Let's learn Hebrew: Fish
* Worksheet: Swallowed by a fish
* Worksheet: Understanding the Hebrew day
* Coloring worksheet: Jonah and the great fish
* Worksheet: Who was Jonah?
* Labyrinth: To Nineveh!
* Worksheet: City of Nineveh

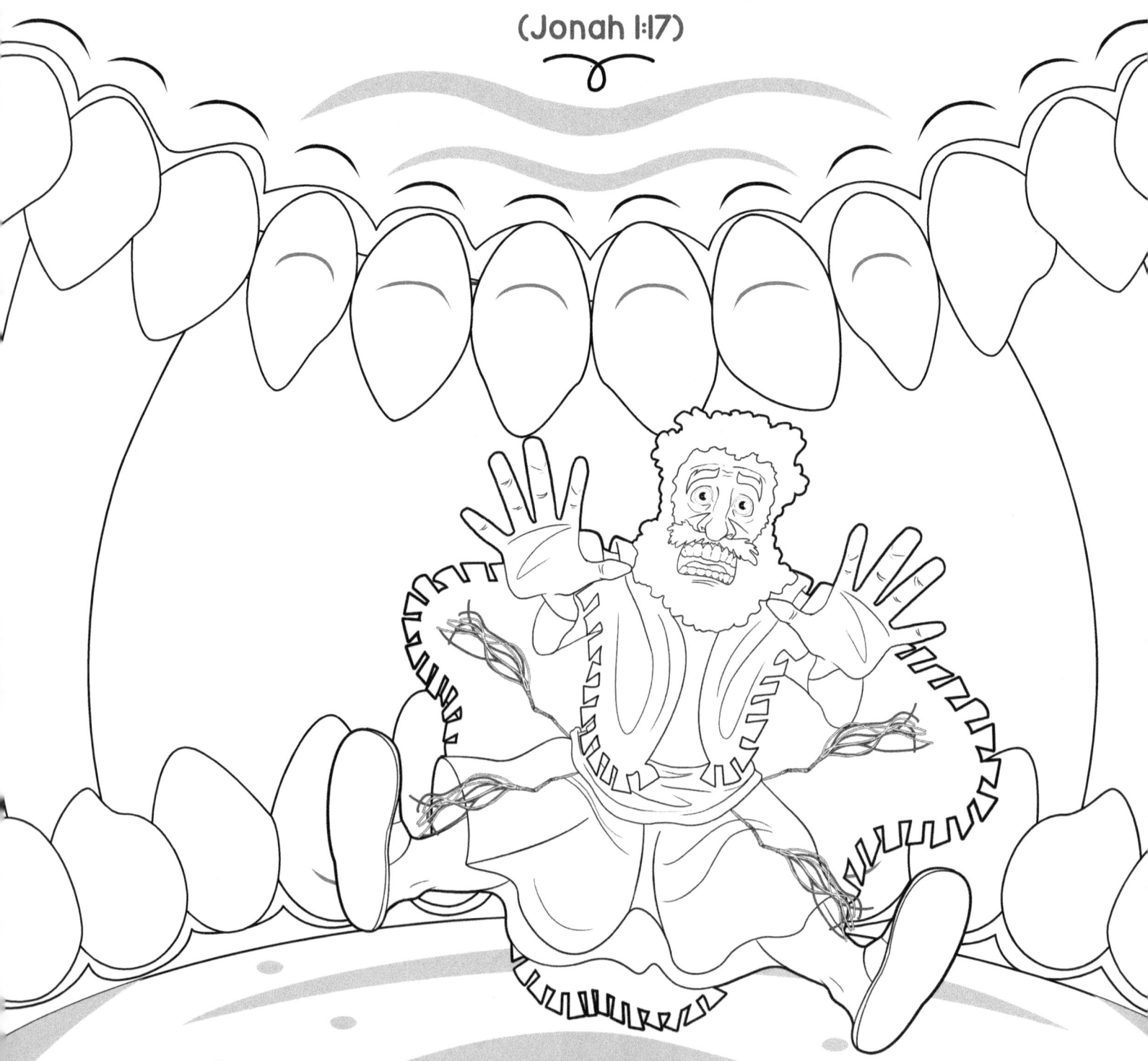

Swallowed by a FISH

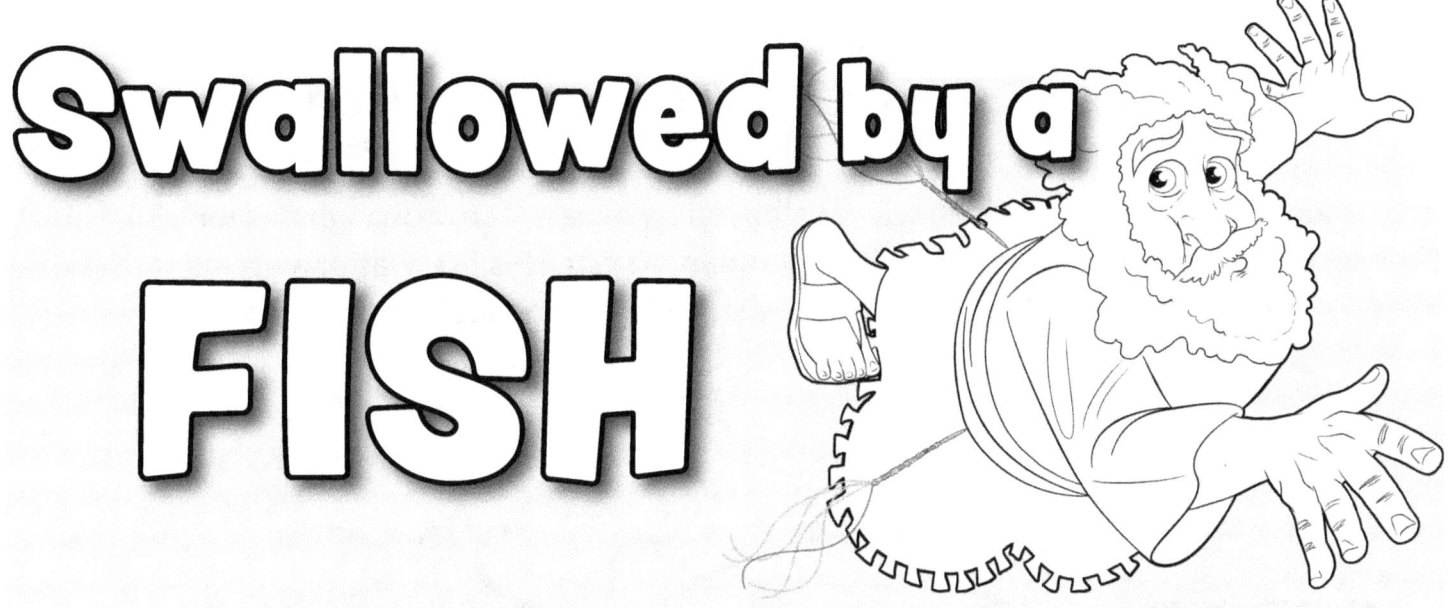

Read Jonah 1:17-3:3. Find and circle the words below.

```
P G Q Y N A W S Q X P X P C X
W R R B P I B A F S G L G I X
S M A E K N I L X M I M Q R M
X A T Y A C P V Z N U O A K R
P J I C E T H A C Q B N N G E
X R U L T R F T S G E U I I P
O R O W O T S I Z I L B N O E
E N U P J R S O S T L V E P N
E J Y N H U S N W H Y R V N T
W M I O T E V X Y K E G E E A
U A M C P Z T C O W Z O H E N
A X T B C X Y I I S B M L I C
W D V E G S R K J I U Q V G E
X E K B R S F M W S Z N N L J
O Q T E M P L E J O N A H Z V
```

PRAYER
SAILORS
PROPHET
BELLY
TEMPLE
SALVATION
JONAH
REPENTANCE
GREAT FISH
NINEVEH
SHEOL
WATER

Parts of a fish

According to the Bible, Jonah was swallowed by a great fish, not a whale (Jonah 1:17). The Hebrew word used in the Bible is 'dag', meaning fish. This fish was of a great (gadôl) size. Using the Internet or an encyclopedia, research and label the parts of a fish.

1. mouth
2. eye
3. fin
4. gills
5. tail
6. pectoral fin
7. body

Where did Jonah spend three days and three nights?

....

....

Dag

The Hebrew word for fish is "dag." The fish that swallowed Jonah was described as being of a great (gadôl) size. This story helps teach us about repentance and the importance of following God's instructions. Jonah learned these lessons while he was inside the fish for three days and three nights (Jonah 1:17). In the New Testament, Yeshua, also known as Jesus, performed miracles involving fish, such as when He fed 5,000 people with just five loaves of bread and two fish (Matthew 14:13-21).

Dag

(DAHG)

fish

דָג

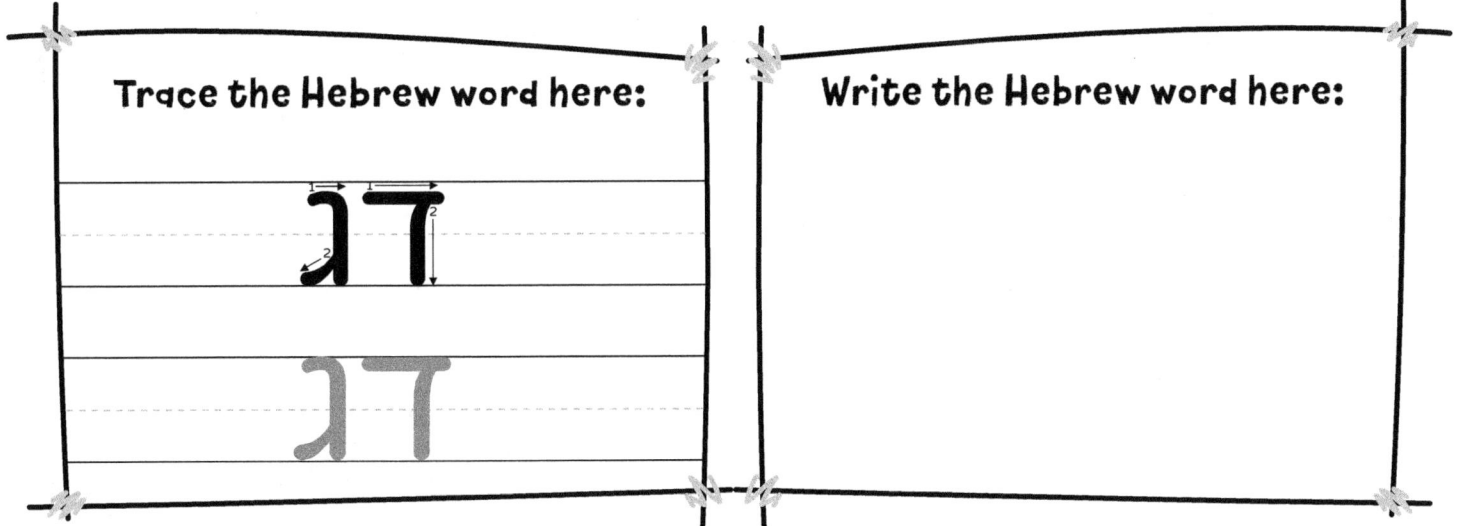

Trace the Hebrew word here:

Write the Hebrew word here:

Swallowed by a fish

What did Jonah eat while he was inside the fish? Use your imagination!

....
....
....
....
....
....
....
....

Imagine you were stuck inside a fish for three days and nights. What would you say to God?

....
....
....
....
....
....
....

This miracle teaches me....

....
....
....
....
....

Draw Jonah inside the great fish.

Understanding the Hebrew day

The Hebrew prophet Jonah was inside a great fish for three days and three nights. In the Hebrew calendar, a day starts at sunset and continues until the next sunset. This is different from the Gregorian calendar we use today, where a day starts and ends at midnight. In the space below, draw a picture of the Hebrew day cycle. Start with the sun setting to show the beginning of the day. Label the different parts: Sunset, Night, Sunrise, Daytime, and Sunset again. Color your drawing to show the transition from night to day.

Sunset

Jonah and the great fish

Read Jonah 1:17 and write the Bible verse below.

....

....

....

1. How long was Jonah inside the belly of the fish?

....

....

2. What did Jonah do while he was inside the fish?

....

....

3. What instructions did God give Jonah?

....

....

Draw your favorite scene from this story.

What lesson could Jonah's initial disobedience teach me?	God used Jonah to...
....	....
....	....

Who was Jonah?

Read 2 Kings 14 and Jonah 1:1-4:11. Complete the worksheet below.

Jonah was the son of .... He came from ....

Jonah was a:

....

God sent Jonah to Nineveh to:

....

Jonah tried to flee to Tarshish because:

....

Jonah is most famous for:

....

....

Five words that describe Jonah:

1. ....
2. ....
3. ....
4. ....
5. ....

To Nineveh!

God told Jonah to go to the city of Nineveh and deliver His message. Help Jonah make his way to Nineveh.

City of Nineveh

Before Nineveh was destroyed in 612 BC, it was the capital of the Assyrian Empire and the largest city in the world. Its location on the main road between the Mediterranean Sea and the Indian Ocean connected Asia with the Middle East. This central location made Nineveh an important business center, and as a result, Nineveh became a very wealthy city. Nineveh was famous for its magnificent buildings. It was there that King Sennacherib (705–681 BC) planned streets and squares, built zoos and temples, and designed the famous "palace without rival." According to building plans discovered in the ruins of Nineveh, this palace had over 80 rooms.

In the mid-1800s, archaeologists found the ruins of Nineveh in modern-day Iraq. The walls and gates can still be seen near the banks of the Tigris River, just opposite the modern city of Mosul. In one of the royal libraries, archaeologists discovered 30,000 cuneiform texts from throughout the Assyrian empire. These clay-tablet documents, including the famous "Epic of Gilgamesh," provided valuable information about ancient Nineveh and its way of life.

Think about life in ancient Nineveh. Answer the questions below.

1. How do you think the central location of Nineveh contributed to its development as a major business center?

2. How do you think the discovery of the 30,000 cuneiform texts in the ruins of Nineveh contribute to our understanding of ancient Assyrian culture?

LESSON FOUR

Nineveh repents: Jonah 3:1-10

1. Lesson objectives:

During this lesson, children will explore:
1. How the people of Nineveh showed their repentance
2. How God showed mercy on the people of Nineveh

2. Introduction:

Start the class by asking your students to imagine they are messengers with an important message that could help people change for the better. Ask them to think about how they would make sure everyone listens and understands. Share a quick example of someone who made a difference by delivering an important message, like a famous leader or activist. This will help students understand the power of sharing a message with purpose. Say, "What do you think happened when Jonah shared God's message with the people of Nineveh? Let's find out!"

3. Review key vocabulary:

- **NINEVEH:** An ancient city in the Middle East

- **REPENTANCE:** Turning back to God and His Ways (Acts 26:20)

- **SACKCLOTH:** A rough, scratchy fabric that people wore to show they were sad, mourning, or in repentance

- **DECREE:** An official order or decision made by someone in charge, like a king or government

- **KING OF NINEVEH:** Some Bible scholars believe that the king of Nineveh was Adad-Nirari III

4. Bible memory verse to help children remember God's Word:

"When God saw what they did, how they turned from their evil way, He relented of the disaster that He said He would do to them…" (Jonah 3:10)

5. Read Jonah 3:1-10 or read the Bible story below:

God spoke to Jonah again and told him, "Go to the great city of Nineveh. Tell them the message I have for you." Jonah listened to God this time and set out for Nineveh. Nineveh was a huge city, so big that it took three days to walk across it. When Jonah arrived, he began to walk through the city, shouting, "In 40 days, Nineveh will be destroyed!" The people of Nineveh heard Jonah's message and believed God. They decided to turn back to God and show their repentance by fasting and wearing sackcloth. Everyone did this, from the most important people to the least. When the king of Nineveh heard Jonah's message, he got up from his throne, took off his royal robes, put on sackcloth, and sat in ashes. Then he made an announcement to everyone in Nineveh: "No one, not even animals, should eat or drink anything. Everyone must wear sackcloth and pray to God. Let everyone turn from his evil way and from the violence that is in his hands. Maybe God will relent and turn from his fierce anger so that we may not perish." When God saw what the people of Nineveh did, He decided not to destroy the city as He had planned. God showed mercy because they turned from their wicked ways.

6. Let's review:

1. What was today's story about?
2. What message did God give to Jonah to deliver to the people of Nineveh?
3. How long did it take to walk across the city of Nineveh?
4. What did the people of Nineveh do to show they were sorry for their actions?
5. What did the king of Nineveh do after hearing Jonah's message?
6. How did God respond to the people of Nineveh when they turned from their wicked ways?

7. Activites:

* Coloring page: The king of Nineveh repents
* Bible quiz: God's message to Nineveh
* Bible word scramble: How big was Nineveh?
* Worksheet: Who was the King of Nineveh?
* Worksheet: Write your name in cuneiform
* Bible activity: Ancient Nineveh
* Worksheet: Sackcloth and ashes
* Worksheet: Repentance in action
* Coloring activity: Discovering the Assyrian King
* Worksheet: Meet the cast

> "Let niether man or animal taste anything; let them not feed or drink water."
>
> (Jonah 3:7)

God's message to NINEVEH

Read Jonah 3:1-10. Answer the questions below.

1. To which city did God ask Jonah to take His message of repentance?

2. How many people lived in this city?

3. How many days did it take to walk across the city?

4. In how many days did Jonah say the city would be overthrown?

5. What did the people do to show they believed God's message?

6. What did the king do to show he had repented?

7. What new command did the king give the people?

8. What did the people of Nineveh hope to achieve by fasting and wearing sackcloth?

9. What did the king of Nineveh hope would happen if they repented?

10. How did God respond when the people of Nineveh turned from their wicked ways?

How big was Nineveh?

Unscramble the words to find the answer. *Hint: Read Jonah 3:3 (ESV).*

"Nineveh was an

exceedingly great city,

three days' journey in

breadth."

Who was the King of Nineveh?

Adad-Nirari III was a king of the Assyrian Empire who ruled from about 805 to 782 BCE. In 1905, an important artifact called the Saba'a Stele was found in the Sinjar Mountains of Syria. This stele, made around 800 BCE, talks about some of Adad-Nirari's military actions, including an attack on the king of Aram and the tribute he received. It also mentions "Palestine" (Pa-la-áš-tu), one of the earliest mentions in archaeological records.

The events on the stele are similar to a Bible story in 2 Kings 13:1-9. This story tells about King Jehoahaz of Israel and how his people were oppressed by the Arameans. The Bible says that God sent a deliverer to help Israel, and some scholars think this could have been Adad-Nirari III. His military campaigns against the Arameans might have lessened the threat to Israel. Adad-Nirari III's reign is also known for a religious change, where Nabu, the god of wisdom, became the main god worshiped. This time period matches with when the prophet Jonah was active, calling Nineveh to repentance. While it's not certain, the idea that Adad-Nirari III's actions and Jonah's influence were connected is an interesting possibility. What do you think?

Read the article above. Answer the questions.

1. How does the Saba'a Stele connect the reign of Adad-Nirari III to the story of King Jehoahaz of Israel in 2 Kings 13:1-9?

2. What are some reasons scholars believe that Adad-Nirari III might have been the unnamed deliverer who helped Israel during its oppression by the Arameans?

Write your name in Cuneiform

Cuneiform is an ancient form of writing that started in Mesopotamia, one of the earliest places where people lived together in cities. It was used by the Assyrians, Babylonians, and Sumerians to write things down. People wrote cuneiform by pressing a pointed stick called a stylus into soft clay tablets, which made wedge-shaped marks. They used it to record things like laws, trades, and stories. This is the type of writing that people used when Jonah was alive.

Write your name in cuneiform:

Ancient Nineveh

Imagine you are a Ninevite. Write a paragraph describing what life was like in Nineveh at the time of Jonah. How did you and your friends react to Jonah's message?

....
....
....
....
....
....
....

Sackcloth and ashes

In ancient times, people used sackcloth and ashes to express deep sorrow and repentance. Sackcloth was a rough, scratchy fabric made from goat or camel hair. Unlike the soft and colorful clothes people typically wore, sackcloth was plain and uncomfortable, symbolizing that someone was truly sorry or grieving. Wearing sackcloth showed others that a person was in mourning or wanted to repent for something they had done wrong. Along with sackcloth, people used ashes to show their sorrow. Ashes are the powdery substance left after burning something, and people would sprinkle them on their heads or sit in them. This was a way to visibly show their sadness or regret, whether they were mourning a loved one or seeking forgiveness for their actions.

In the Bible, the people of Nineveh wore sackcloth and sat in ashes after hearing Jonah's message from God. They wanted to demonstrate their repentance and hoped for forgiveness. This tradition of using sackcloth and ashes allowed ancient people like the Ninevites to express their emotions and show a desire to turn back to Yahweh, the God of Abraham, Isaac, and Jacob.

Draw the king of Nineveh in repentance.

Repentance in action

Repentance means turning back to God and following His ways. The Bible says, "I preached that they should repent and turn to God and prove their repentance by their deeds" (Acts 26:20). To show God they had repented, the Ninevites wore sackcloth. This was a coarse, black cloth made from goat's hair and worn with burnt ashes as a sign of repentance. Although the people of Nineveh repented after Jonah preached, their children didn't follow God's ways. One hundred years later, the prophet Nahum warned that God would destroy Nineveh because the people were so wicked. Sure enough, Nineveh was completely destroyed by the armies of the Median and Babylonian empires in 612 BC.

Read the article above. Answer the questions.

1. What is repentance?
   ....
   ....

2. Describe how you demonstrate you are in repentance?
   ....
   ....
   ....
   ....
   ....
   ....
   ....
   ....

Discovering the Assyrian King

Unlike the ancient Egyptians, the Assyrians did not think their king was a god. Instead, they saw him as the helper of their main god, Ashur, and his representative on Earth. The king's job was to make Assyria bigger and to bring order and civilization to places that needed it. Draw the right side of the king as a mirror image of the left side.

Meet the cast

Read Jonah 1:1-3:10. The story of Jonah features four important Bible characters: Jonah, the sailors, the king of Nineveh, and a great fish. For each character, fill in information about their role in the story.

Role: ....
....
....

JONAH

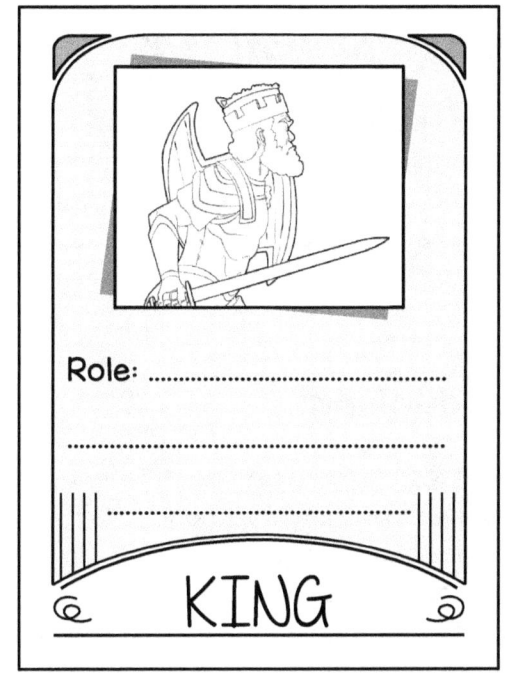

Role: ....
....
....

KING

Role: ....
....
....

CAPTAIN

Role: ....
....
....

GREAT FISH

LESSON FIVE

Jonah and the plant: Jonah 4:1-11

1. Lesson objectives:

During this lesson, children will explore:
1. How Jonah responded to God's mercy toward the people of Nineveh
2. How God taught Jonah a lesson about mercy

2. Introduction:

To begin the lesson, hold up two different-sized empty jars, one large and one small. Ask your students to imagine the large jar represents God's mercy and the small jar represents human mercy. Explain that God's mercy is vast and limitless, while our human mercy can sometimes be small or limited. Ask students to think about a time when they needed to show mercy to someone else. Then introduce today's lesson, where Jonah struggles to understand God's great mercy toward the people of Nineveh. Say, "Let's find out how God taught Jonah an important lesson about mercy."

3. Review key vocabulary:

- **NINEVEH:** An ancient city in the Middle East

- **ANGRY:** A strong feeling you have when something is not fair or when someone is mean to you

- **PLANT:** Bible scholars suggest this was a castor oil plant, which is a tall leafy plant that grows quickly

- **FAINT:** A moment when you suddenly feel weak and lose consciousness for a short time

- **WITHERED:** When a plant or flower dries up and shrinks because it doesn't have enough water

4. Bible memory verse to help children remember God's Word:

"God appointed a plant and made it come up over Jonah, that it might be a shade over his head..." (Jonah 4:6)

5. Read Jonah 4:1-11 or read the Bible story below:

Jonah was upset and angry with God. He prayed and said, "God, I knew this would happen! That's why I tried to run away to Tarshish. I knew you are a kind and loving God, slow to get angry and full of love. You don't want to punish people. Now, please take my life, because I'd rather die than see this." God replied, "Do you have a good reason to be angry?" Jonah left the city and sat down to the east of it. He made a small shelter to sit under and waited to see what would happen to the city. God made a plant grow up over Jonah to give him shade and make him feel better. Jonah was very happy about the plant. But the next morning, God sent a worm to attack the plant, and it dried up. When the sun rose, God sent a hot wind, and the sun beat down on Jonah's head. He felt faint and wished he could die, saying, "I'd rather die than live." God asked Jonah, "Do you have a good reason to be angry about the plant?" Jonah answered, "Yes, I'm so angry I could die." God said, "You care about the plant, but you didn't make it grow. It came up in one night and died in another. Shouldn't I care about Nineveh, that big city with more than 120,000 people who don't know right from wrong, and all the animals too?"

6. Let's review:

1. What was today's story about?
2. Why was Jonah upset and angry with God?
3. What did Jonah do after leaving the city of Nineveh?
4. How did God help Jonah while he was sitting outside the city?
5. What happened to the plant that shaded Jonah?
6. How did Jonah feel when the plant died?
7. What lesson did God want Jonah to learn from the plant?

7. Activites:

* Coloring page: Jonah and the plant
* Newspaper worksheet: Nineveh repents!
* Bible crossword puzzle: Jonah in Nineveh
* Worksheet: From shade to sun
* Worksheet: How do plants grow?
* Let's learn Hebrew: Tola'at
* Worksheet: Design a worm
* Bible activity: God is merciful
* Worksheet: Exploring mercy
* Bible quiz: Jonah and the big fish
* Story sequencing activity: Jonah's big adventure
* Worksheet: True or false?
* Bible story worksheets: Write your own story of Jonah

"Jonah sat in the shade, till he should see what would become of the city."
(Jonah 4:5)

City of Nineveh

The Nineveh Times

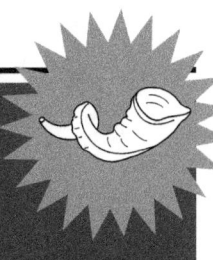

MESOPOTAMIA   A BIBLE HISTORY PUBLICATION

Prophet visits city   # Nineveh repents!

....
....
....
....
....
....

Plants for sale

Jonah in NINEVEH

Read Jonah 3:10-4:11 (ESV). Complete the crossword below.

ACROSS

1) "Should not I _____ Nineveh in which there are more than 120,000 persons…" (Jonah 4:11)
2) God sent a worm to attack the plant at this time.
4) The strong wind God sent, causing Jonah discomfort.
7) The plant that God provided for Jonah's comfort.
8) Jonah was this when the plant withered.
9) Jonah was upset because God showed this to Nineveh.

DOWN

1) Jonah wanted to die rather than live without this.
3) The city Jonah was sent to by God.
5) Jonah made a shelter and sat in its _____.
6) The number of days Jonah said Nineveh would be overthrown.

From shade to sun

In Jonah 4:1-11, God used a castor-bean plant to teach Jonah a lesson about mercy. This plant grows quickly and can become as big as a small tree, with very large green leaves. Originally, it grew in regions like the southeastern Mediterranean, eastern Africa, and India, but now it is found in tropical areas all over the world. Create a storyboard to illustrate how God used the castor bean plant to teach Jonah about mercy. Draw a series of pictures showing Jonah sitting under the plant, the plant providing shade, and then the plant withering away. Below each picture, write a caption to help you explain the lesson of mercy.

Tola'at

The Hebrew word for worm is Tola'at. Worms are mentioned in the Bible in several stories and often represent things like decay or smallness. In the story of Jonah, God sent a worm to eat a plant that gave Jonah shade. This taught Jonah a lesson about mercy and caring for others (Jonah 4:7). In other parts of the Bible, like in Isaiah 14:11, worms are used to show how even powerful people can become weak and humble. In Job 25:6, worms are used to remind people to be humble and remember that everyone is small compared to God.

Tola'at
(Toh-LAH-aht)

worm

תוֹלַעַת

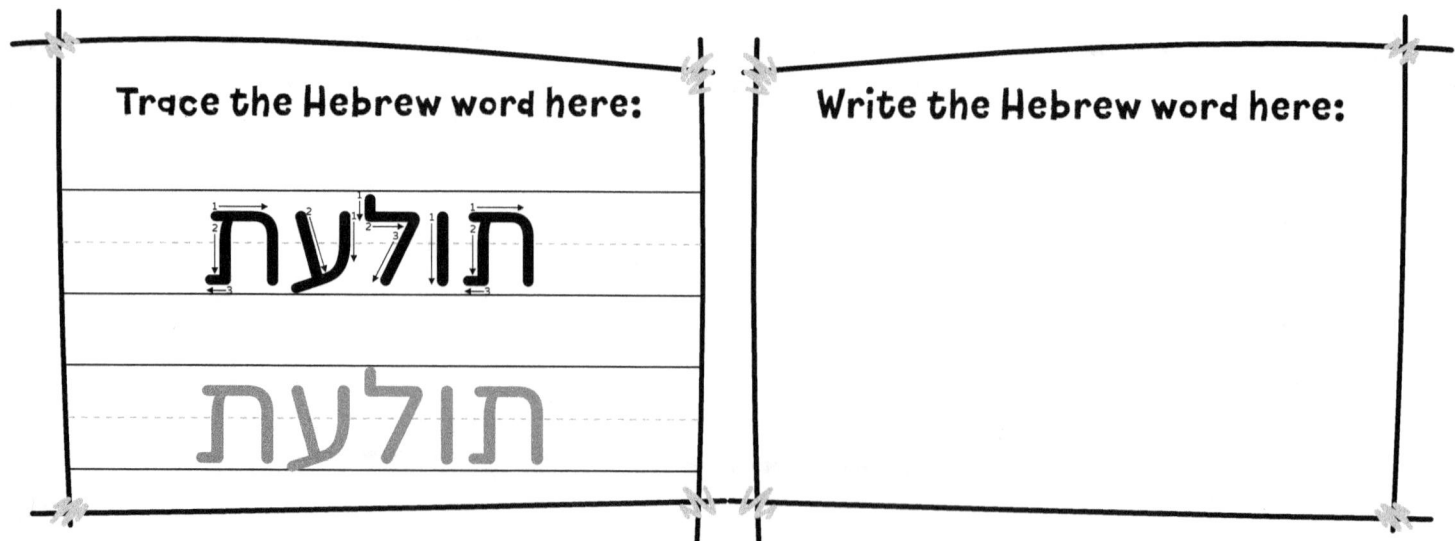

Trace the Hebrew word here:

Write the Hebrew word here:

Design a worm

In Jonah 4:1-11, God sent a worm to eat the plant that provided Jonah with shade. In the space below, use your imagination to create your own unique worm. Draw and color your worm, and give it a name.

Design your own worm!

What do I like to eat?

Exploring mercy

God taught Jonah a lesson about mercy. How did He do this?
Read Jonah 4:1-11 and write a short summary below.

Answer the questions below.

What was Jonah's reaction to God sparing Nineveh?

How did God demonstrate His mercy to Nineveh, despite Jonah's anger?

What lesson did God teach Jonah through the plant?

Bible Pathway Adventures

Jonah and the BIG FISH

Read Jonah 1:1-4:11. Answer the questions below.

1. To which city did God ask Jonah to take His message of repentance?

2. Where did Jonah try to run to instead of going to Nineveh?

3. In which city did Jonah board a ship?

4. What did Jonah do during the storm?

5. Who threw Jonah overboard?

6. What happened after Jonah was thrown overboard?

7. How long was Jonah inside the fish?

8. Where did Jonah go after reaching dry land?

9. What did Jonah tell the people when he reached Nineveh?

10. What killed the plant that God had provided Jonah for shade?

Jonah's big adventure

Read Jonah 1:1-4:11 and review the ten sentences below. They recount the story of Jonah, but they're out of order! Your task is to arrange the sentences correctly. Write a number next to each sentence to sequence the events in their proper order.

A. .... To calm the storm, the sailors threw Jonah overboard into the sea.

B. .... Jonah prayed to God while he was in the fish, and God made the fish spit him out onto dry land.

C. .... While Jonah was on the ship, God sent a big storm.

D. .... Jonah told the sailors that the storm was his fault because he was running away from God.

E. .... The people of Nineveh listened to Jonah, repented, and God decided to spare their city.

F. .... God told Jonah to go to the city of Nineveh and tell the people to repent.

G. .... God sent a great fish to swallow Jonah, and he was inside the fish for three days and three nights.

H. .... Jonah obeyed God and went to Nineveh, warning the people that their city would be destroyed in forty days if they did not repent.

I. .... Jonah was upset that God showed mercy to Nineveh, but God taught him a lesson about compassion through the example of a plant.

J. .... Instead of obeying God, Jonah tried to run away and boarded a ship heading to Tarshish.

True or false?

Are the statements below TRUE or FALSE?
Read Jonah 1:1-4:11. Circle the correct box below.

Jonah was a prophet.	TRUE	FALSE
Jonah boarded a raft to Tarshish.	TRUE	FALSE
Jonah stayed inside the fish for four days and four nights.	TRUE	FALSE
Jonah told the Ninevites to repent.	TRUE	FALSE
The king of Nineveh wore sackcloth and sat in ashes.	TRUE	FALSE
More than 1,000,000 people lived in Nineveh.	TRUE	FALSE

Are these statements true or false?

Write your own story of Jonah

Read Jonah 1:1-4:11.
Beside each picture, write in your own words the story of Jonah. Color the pictures.

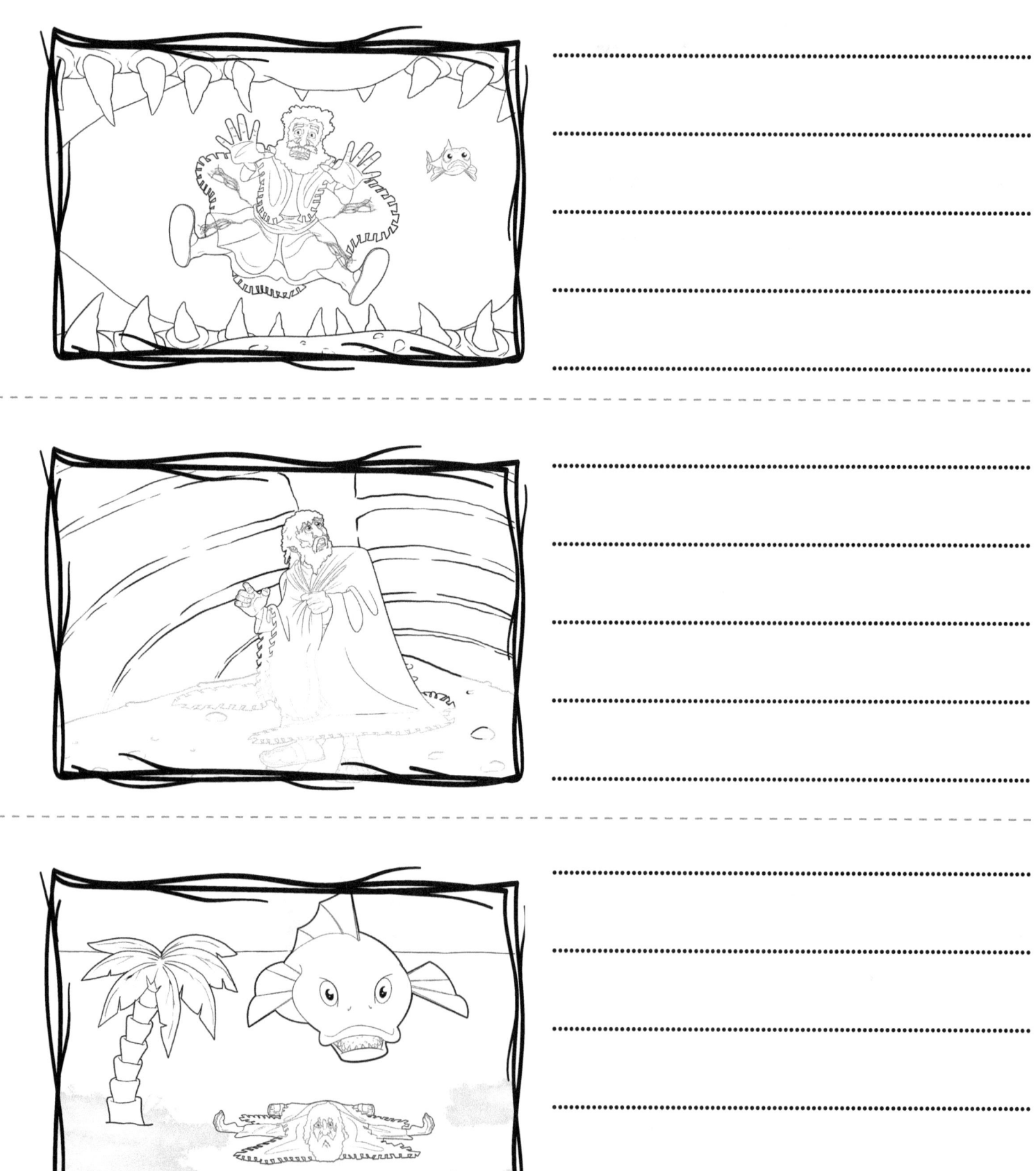

Bible Pathway Adventures

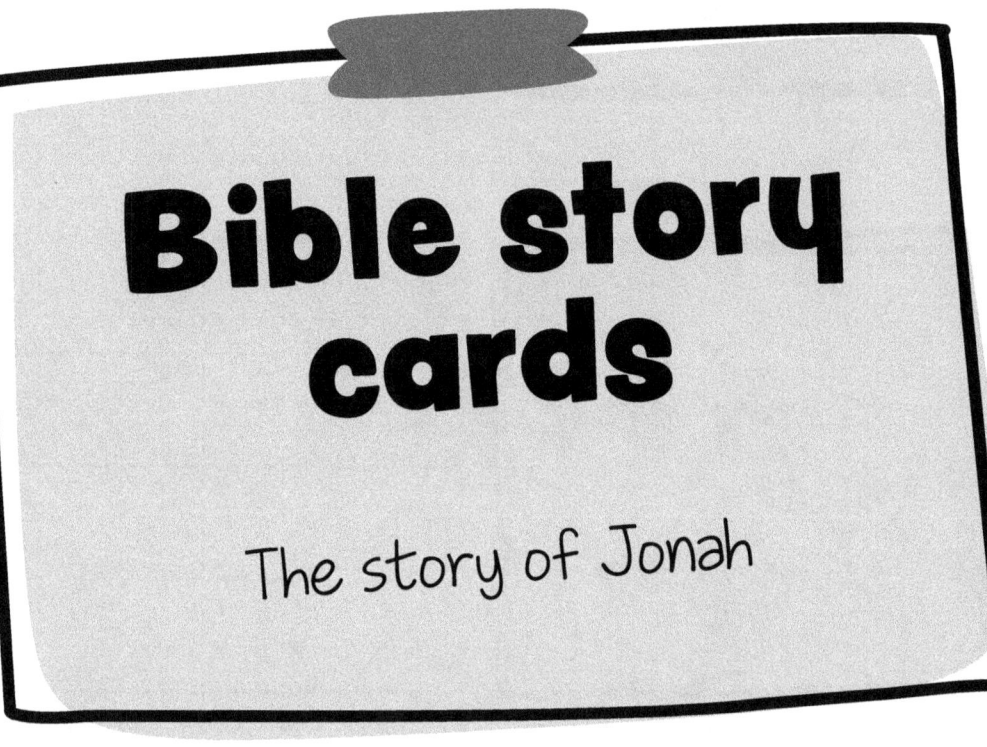

Bible story cards

The story of Jonah

The Call of Jonah

"Arise, go to Nineveh, that great city, and call out against it, for their evil has come up before Me."

Jonah 1:2

 Jonah 1:1-3

Storm at Sea

God hurled a great wind upon the sea, and there was a mighty tempest on the sea, so that the ship threatened to break up.

Jonah 1:4

 Jonah 1:4-6

Jonah's Confession

Jonah said to the sailors, "I am a Hebrew, and I fear Yahweh, the God of heaven, who made the sea and the dry land."

Jonah 1:9

 Jonah 1:7-10

Overboard!

The sailors picked up Jonah and hurled him into the sea, and the sea ceased from its raging.

Jonah 1:15

 Jonah 1:11-16

Swallowed by a Fish

God appointed a great fish to swallow up Jonah. And Jonah was in the belly of the fish three days and three nights.

Jonah 1:17

 Jonah 1:17

Jonah Repents

"But I with the voice of thanksgiving will sacrifice to you; what I have vowed I will pay. Salvation belongs to God!"

Jonah 2:9

 Jonah 2:1-9

On Dry Land

God spoke to the great fish, and it vomited Jonah out upon the dry land.

Jonah 2:10

 Jonah 2:10

Jonah Goes to Nineveh

Jonah arose and went to Nineveh, according to the word of God. Nineveh was an exceedingly great city three days' journey in breadth.

Jonah 3:3

 Jonah 3:1-4

Nineveh Repentance

The people of Nineveh believed God. They called for a fast and put on sackcloth, from the greatest of them to the least of them.

Jonah 3:5

 Jonah 3:5-9

God's Mercy

When God saw what they did, how they turned from their evil way, He relented of the disaster that he had said he would do to them, and he did not do it.

Jonah 3:10

 Jonah 3:10

Jonah's Shelter

Jonah went out of the city and sat to the east of the city and made a booth for himself there. He sat under it in the shade, till he should see what would become of the city.

Jonah 4:5

 Jonah 4:1-6

God Appoints a Worm

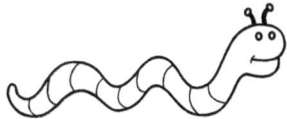

But when dawn came up the next day, God appointed a worm that attacked the plant, so that it withered.

Jonah 4:7

 Jonah 4:7-11

Crafts & Projects

Jonah sails to Tarshish

Jonah tried to sail to Tarshish.
Color and cut out Jonah and the men. Place them inside the ship.

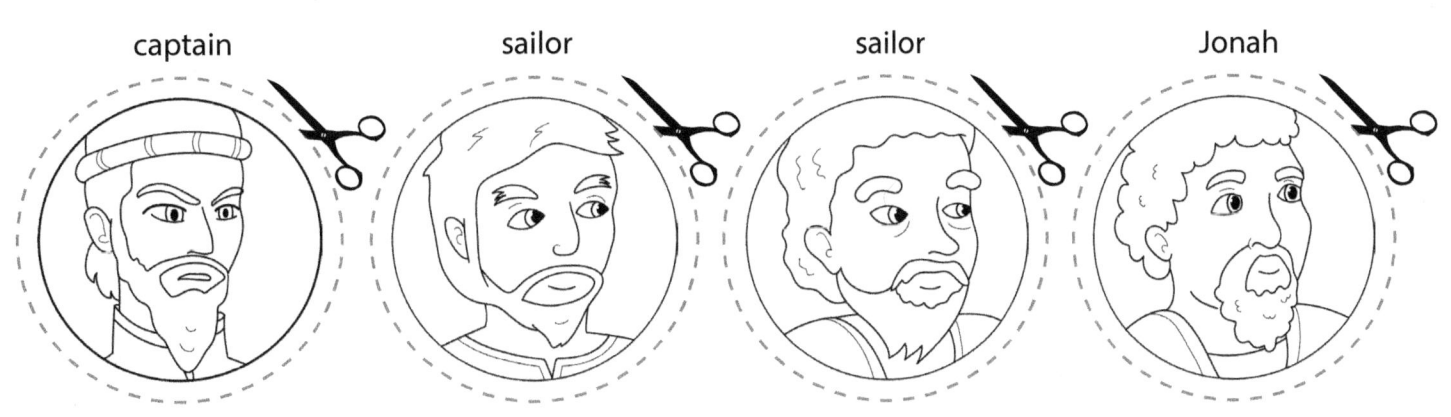

captain   sailor   sailor   Jonah

Make a rain cloud

You will need:

1. White and blue cardstock
2. Cotton balls
3. Paper plate
4. Yellow paint or crayons
5. School glue, glue stick, and clear tape
6. String or yarn

Instructions:

1. Copy or print the templates onto white and blue cardstock. Cut out the cloud and raindrops.
2. Glue or tape four pieces of string onto the back of the cloud. Tape three blue raindrops onto each piece of string, spacing them evenly.
3. Color the paper plate yellow. When the plate is dry, cut out the sun rays. Then cut the bottom sun rays from the sun to make it easier to glue the sun to the cloud.
4. Glue the sun to the cloud. Cover the cloud in glue and add cotton balls to make your cloud fluffy.

How do plants grow?

Color and cut out the different stages of the plant life cycle.
Paste them onto the page in the correct order.

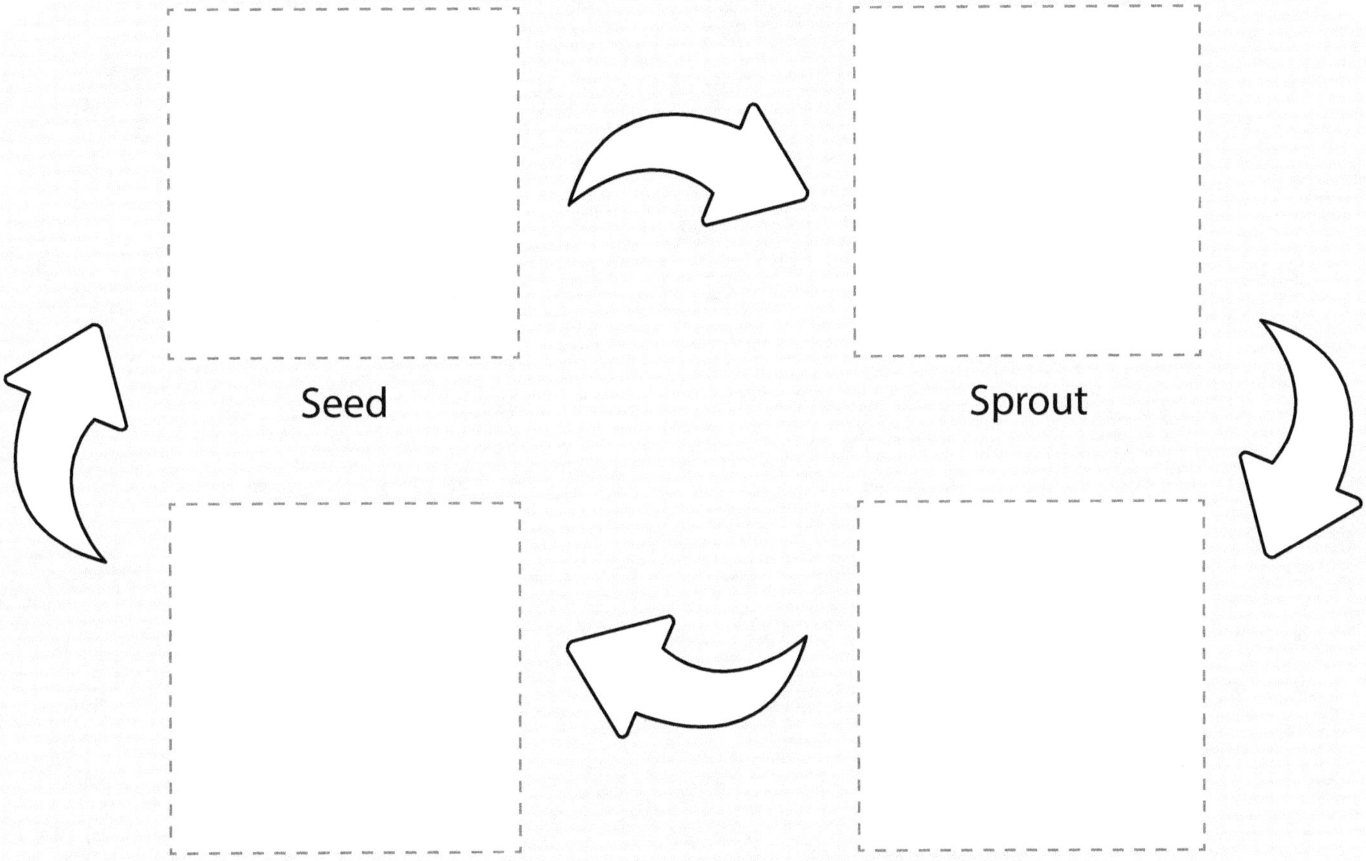

Seed

Sprout

Plant

Seedling

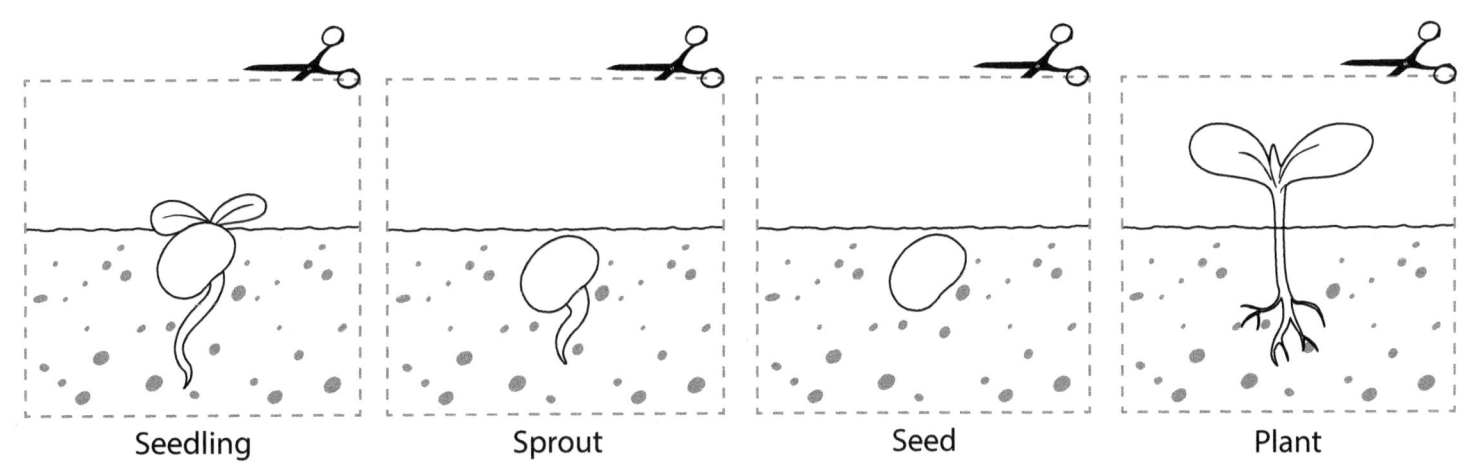

Seedling   Sprout   Seed   Plant

God is merciful

Jonah waited outside the city to see what God would do.
Color and cut out Jonah and the objects. Paste them onto the page.

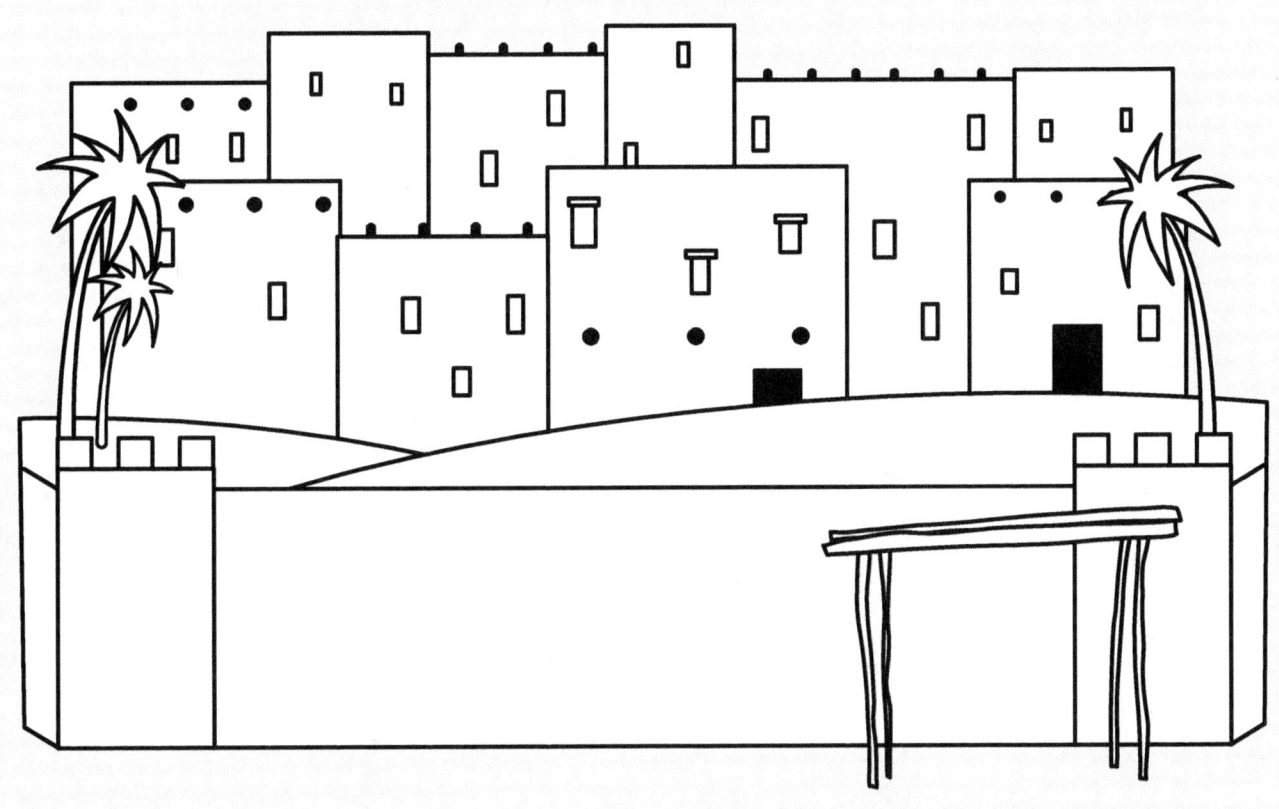

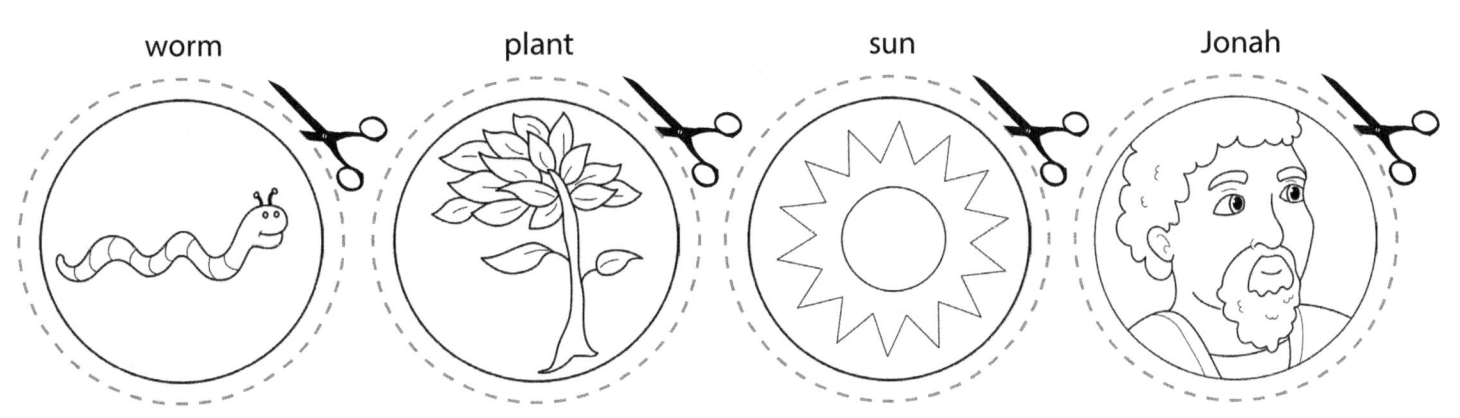

worm   plant   sun   Jonah

www.biblepathwayadventures.com
Jonah and the Big Fish Activity Book

© BPA Publishing Ltd 2024

ANSWER KEY

Lesson One: The runaway prophet
Let's Review:
1. The story was about Jonah trying to run away from God
2. God spoke to Jonah, the son of Amittai
3. God told Jonah to go to Nineveh and tell the people to stop doing bad things
4. Jonah went to Joppa and got on a ship going to Tarshish
5. Jonah decided to run away because he didn't want to go to Nineveh
6. A prophet is a person called by God to speak for Him

Bible word search: The runaway prophet

Worksheet: The port of Joppa
1. Joppa was an ideal port because it was located on the eastern Mediterranean coast and had a natural harbor, making it a perfect spot for ships to anchor safely. This made it a bustling hub for trade and travel
2. Jonah likely chose to go to Joppa to find a ship because it was a well-known and busy port with many Phoenician ships preparing for long voyages
3. The Phoenicians' skills in navigation and trade allowed them to set up extensive trade routes connecting places like Egypt, Cyprus, and other important locations. Their ability to travel long distances across the Mediterranean Sea helped them spread goods, ideas, and culture, increasing their influence across the region

Worksheet: What's the Word?
The word of Yahweh came to Jonah, son of Amittai: "Go to the great city of Nineveh and preach against it, because its wickedness has come up before Me." But Jonah ran away from God and headed for Tarshish. He went down to Joppa where he found a ship bound for that port. After paying the fare, he went aboard and sailed for Tarshish to flee from God. Then God sent a great wind on the sea, and such a violent storm arose that the ship threatened to break up.

Worksheet: Jonah runs from God
1. God told Jonah to go to Nineveh to preach against its wickedness and urge the people to repent
2. Jonah likely disobeyed God because he was afraid or unwilling to carry out God's instruction, possibly fearing the reaction of the people of Nineveh
3. Jonah boarded a ship at the port of Joppa (modern-day Jaffa)

Worksheet: Discovering the tribe of Zebulun
1. Zebulun was the tenth son of Jacob and the founder of one of the twelve tribes of Israel
2. The tribe of Zebulun settled in a small portion of southern Galilee, between Asher and Naphtali
3. Jonah was of the tribe of Zebulun
4. Deborah praised the tribe of Zebulun for risking their lives

Worksheet: The land of Zebulun
The tribe of Zebulun was significant in the history of Israel for several reasons: In Judges 5, the people of Zebulun were praised for their bravery and willingness to risk their lives in battle. 1 Chronicles 12 highlights how the tribe provided a large number of seasoned troops to support King David, showcasing their military strength and loyalty. In Isaiah 9, the land of Zebulun is mentioned in a prophecy about the coming of the Messiah, indicating its importance in God's plan for Israel. Finally, in Matthew 4, Yeshua began His ministry in the region of Galilee, where the tribe of Zebulun was located

Lesson Two: Storm at sea
Let's Review:
1. Today's story was about Jonah and the storm sent by God
2. God sent a storm on the sea because Jonah was trying to run away from Him
3. The sailors were scared and cried out to their own gods. They also threw the ship's cargo into the sea to make the ship lighter
4. Jonah was asleep in the inner part of the ship when the storm hit

5. The captain told Jonah to get up and call on his god to save them
6. The sailors decided to cast lots to find out who was responsible for the storm
7. Jonah told the sailors that he was a Hebrew who worshiped Yahweh, the God of heaven, who made the sea and the land, and that he was running away from God
8. Jonah told the sailors to pick him up and throw him into the sea to calm the storm. When they did, the sea became calm

Bible quiz: Jonah and the mighty storm
1. God sent a great wind that caused a mighty storm on the sea
2. The sailors were afraid and each cried out to his own god
3. They threw the ship's cargo into the sea to lighten it
4. Jonah had gone down into the inner part of the ship and was fast asleep
5. The captain told Jonah to get up and call on his god to save them
6. The sailors cast lots to find out who was responsible for the storm, and the lot fell on Jonah
7. Jonah said he was a Hebrew who feared Yahweh, the God of heaven, who made the sea and the dry land
8. The sailors were afraid because Jonah was fleeing from the presence of God
9. Jonah suggested they pick him up and throw him into the sea to calm the storm
10. After the sailors threw Jonah into the sea, the sea became calm

Bible verse puzzle: Who was Jonah?
"I am a Hebrew, and I fear the Lord, the God of heaven, who made the sea and the dry land." (Jonah 1:9)

Lesson Three: Swallowed by a fish
Let's Review:
1. Today's story was about Jonah being swallowed by a great fish, repentance, and then being sent to Nineveh
2. Jonah was inside the belly of the great fish for three days and three nights
3. While he was inside the fish, Jonah prayed to God and repented
4. When Jonah was in trouble, he called out to God for help, and God answered him
5. God told Jonah to go to the city of Nineveh and deliver the message He gave him
6. God sent Jonah to the city of Nineveh after he was spit out by the great fish

Bible word search puzzle: Swallowed by a fish

Coloring worksheet: Jonah and the great fish
1. Jonah was inside the belly of the great fish for three days and three nights
2. While he was inside the great fish, Jonah prayed to God and repented
3. God told Jonah to go to the city of Nineveh and deliver the message He gave him

Worksheet: Who was Jonah?
1. Jonah was the son of Amittai. He came from Gath-hepher (in Zebulun)
2. Jonah was a Hebrew prophet of God
3. God sent Jonah to Nineveh to preach repentance
4. Jonah tried to flee to Tarshish because he didn't want to preach repentance in Nineveh
5. Ask children to answer this question. Answers may vary
6. Ask children to answer this question. Answers may vary

Lesson Four: Nineveh repents
Let's Review:
1. Today's story was about Jonah going to Nineveh to deliver God's message and how the people of Nineveh repented
2. God told Jonah to deliver the message that Nineveh would be destroyed in 40 days unless they changed their ways
3. It took three days to walk across the city of Nineveh
4. The people of Nineveh showed they were sorry by fasting and wearing sackcloth
5. After hearing Jonah's message, the king of Nineveh took off his royal robes, put on sackcloth, and sat in ashes
6. When the people of Nineveh turned from their wicked ways, God showed mercy and decided not to destroy the city as He had planned

Bible quiz: God's message to Nineveh
1. God asked Jonah to take His message of repentance to the city of Nineveh
2. The Bible does not specify the exact number, but it implies a large population by saying there were more than 120,000 people
3. It took three days to walk across the city of Nineveh
4. Jonah said the city would be overthrown in 40 days
5. The people of Nineveh showed they believed God's message by fasting and wearing sackcloth
6. The king of Nineveh showed he had repented by taking off his royal robes, putting on sackcloth, and sitting in ashes
7. The king commanded everyone, including animals, to fast, wear sackcloth, and pray to God
8. The people of Nineveh hoped to achieve God's mercy and avoid destruction by repenting
9. The king of Nineveh hoped that if they repented, God might relent and turn from His fierce anger so they would not perish
10. God responded by showing mercy and deciding not to destroy the city because the people of Nineveh turned from their wicked ways

Bible word scramble: How big was Nineveh?
"Nineveh was an exceedingly great city, three days' journey in breadth." (Jonah 3:3)

Worksheet: Who was the King of Nineveh?
1. The Saba'a Stele describes Adad-Nirari III's military campaigns against the king of Aram, which parallels the Biblical account in 2 Kings 13, where Israel was oppressed by the Arameans and later delivered by an unnamed helper. The timing of Adad-Nirari III's actions aligns with the period of King Jehoahaz's reign
2. Scholars believe Adad-Nirari III might have been the unnamed deliverer because his military campaigns against the Arameans coincided with the Biblical account of Israel's relief from oppression. His actions could have indirectly eased the Aramean threat to Israel, aligning with the Biblical description of a deliverer who helped save Israel from its enemies

Worksheet: Repentance in action
Repentance is turning to God and following His Ways (commands). The Bible says, "I preached that they should repent and turn to God and prove their repentance by their deeds." (Acts 26:20)

Lesson Five: Jonah and the plant
Let's Review:
1. Today's story was about Jonah being upset with God for showing mercy to the people of Nineveh and God's lesson to Jonah through a plant
2. Jonah was upset and angry with God because he did not want God to show mercy and forgive the people of Nineveh
3. After leaving the city of Nineveh, Jonah sat to the east of the city and made a shelter for himself, waiting to see what would happen to the city
4. God helped Jonah by providing a plant that grew to give him shade and make him more comfortable
5. The plant that shaded Jonah withered and died after a worm attacked it the next day
6. Jonah was very angry and upset when the plant died, wishing he could die
7. God wanted Jonah to learn that He cares for all people and that Jonah should have compassion, just as God showed compassion for Nineveh

Bible crossword: Jonah in Nineveh

Worksheet: Exploring mercy
1. Jonah was angry and upset that God spared Nineveh. He felt that it would be better for him to die than to see God show compassion to the city
2. God demonstrated His mercy to Nineveh by sparing the city from destruction. He pitied the people and the animals, recognizing that they did not know their right hand from their left, and decided to relent from sending disaster
3. God taught Jonah a lesson about compassion and perspective through the plant. Jonah felt pity for the plant when it perished, despite not having created or cared for it. God used this to show Jonah that if he could pity a plant, then God could surely have mercy on Nineveh, a city with many people and animals

Bible quiz: Jonah and the big fish
1. God asked Jonah to deliver His message of repentance to the great city of Nineveh
2. Jonah attempted to flee to the distant city of Tarshish to escape from God's command
3. Jonah boarded a ship in the port city of Joppa, intending to sail away to Tarshish instead of going to Nineveh
4. During the violent storm, Jonah was asleep in the lower part of the ship while the sailors were panicking and praying
5. The sailors threw Jonah overboard after casting lots and discovering that he was the cause of the storm
6. Once Jonah was thrown overboard, the storm ceased immediately, and a great fish swallowed him
7. Jonah was inside the belly of the fish for three days and three nights before being spat out onto dry land
8. After reaching dry land, Jonah finally went to Nineveh as God had originally commanded him
9. Jonah warned the people of Nineveh that they had 40 days to repent before their city would be destroyed
10. A worm sent by God attacked the plant, causing it to wither and die, removing the shade it provided Jonah

Story sequencing activity: Jonah's big adventure
1. God told Jonah to go to the city of Nineveh and tell the people to repent.
2. Instead of obeying God, Jonah tried to run away and boarded a ship heading to Tarshish.
3. While Jonah was on the ship, God sent a big storm.
4. Jonah told the sailors that the storm was his fault because he was running away from God.
5. To calm the storm, the sailors threw Jonah overboard into the sea.
6. God sent a great fish to swallow Jonah, and he was inside the fish for three days and three nights.
7. Jonah prayed to God while he was in the fish, and God made the fish spit him out onto dry land.
8. Jonah obeyed God and went to Nineveh, warning the people that their city would be destroyed in forty days if they did not repent.
9. The people of Nineveh listened to Jonah, repented, and God decided to spare their city.
10. Jonah was upset that God showed mercy to Nineveh, but God taught him a lesson about compassion through the example of a plant.

Worksheet: True or false?
Jonah was a prophet (true)
Jonah boarded a raft to Tarshish (false)
Jonah stayed inside the fish for four days and four nights (false)
Jonah told the Ninevites to repent (true)
The king of Nineveh wore sackcloth and sat in ashes (true)
More than 1,000,000 people lived in Nineveh (false)

◈ Discover more Activity Books! ◈

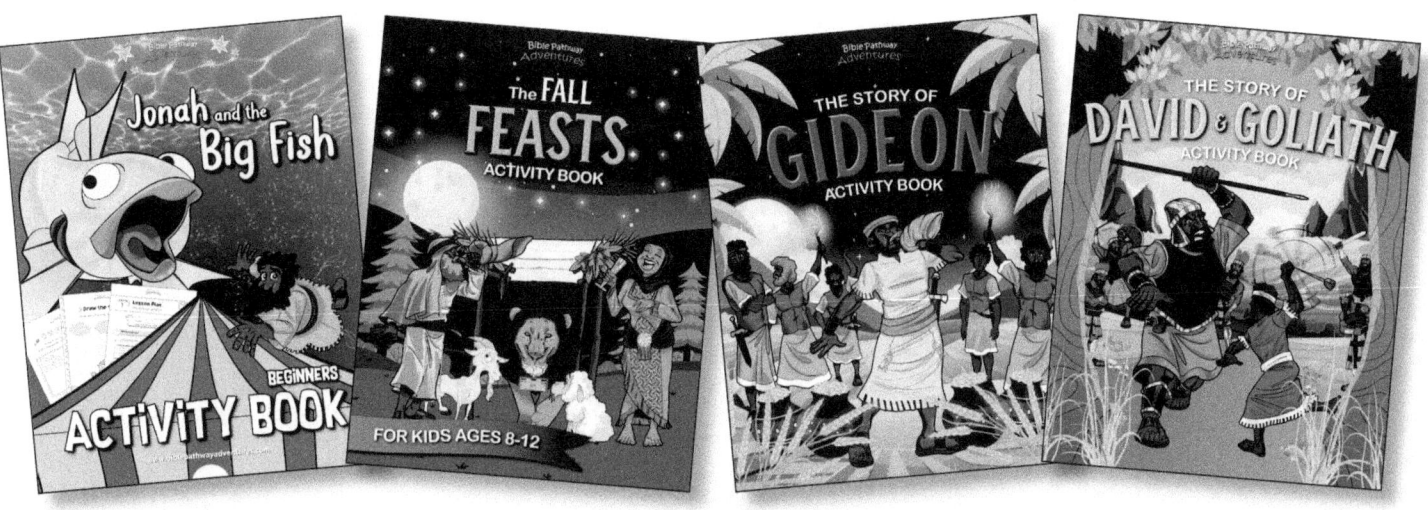

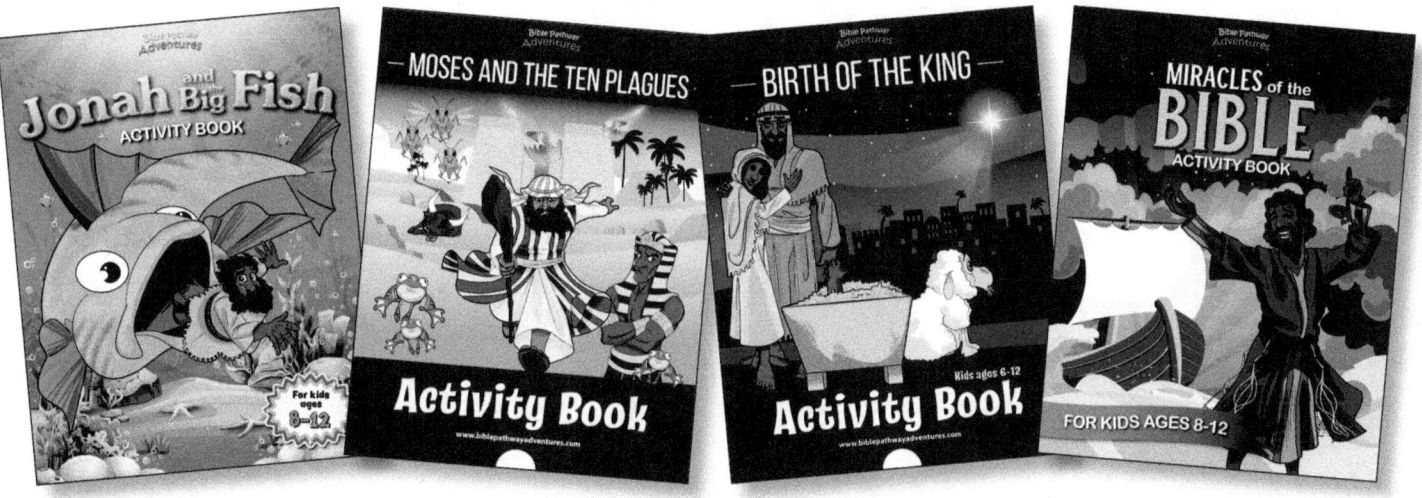

Available for purchase at www.biblepathwayadventures.com

INSTANT DOWNLOAD!

Jonah and the Big Fish (Beginners)
The Fall Feasts
The story of Gideon
The story of David & Goliaths

Jonah and the Big Fish
Moses Ten Plagues
Birth of The King
Bible Miracles

www.ingramcontent.com/pod-product-compliance
Lightning Source LLC
LaVergne TN
LVHW081530060526
838200LV00049B/2270